# The
# GENERAL
## *in the*
# GARDEN

## GEORGE WASHINGTON'S
## LANDSCAPE
## AT MOUNT VERNON

*Foreword by* ANDREA WULF

*Essays by* ADAM T. ERBY, J. DEAN NORTON, *and*
ESTHER C. WHITE

SUSAN P. SCHOELWER, *Editor*

FRED W. SMITH NATIONAL LIBRARY FOR THE STUDY OF GEORGE WASHINGTON
*for the* MOUNT VERNON LADIES' ASSOCIATION

Distributed by the University of Virginia Press

PUBLICATION OF

*The General in the Garden:*

*George Washington's Landscape at Mount Vernon*

HAS BEEN MADE POSSIBLE BY

FUNDING GENEROUSLY PROVIDED BY

Nimick Forbesway Foundation

The Life Guard Society of Historic Mount Vernon

David Bruce Smith Book Fund

———————————————————

FUNDING FOR THE ASSOCIATED EXHIBITION

WAS GENEROUSLY PROVIDED BY

The Life Guard Society of Historic Mount Vernon

Dr. Scholl Foundation

Nimick Forbesway Foundation

Stella Boyle Smith Trust

Neighborhood Friends of Mount Vernon

Anonymous Donor

# Contents

# Foreword

## Andrea Wulf

As a historian, I spend a lot of time in archives and libraries, reading magnificent old books or trying to decipher manuscripts that might reveal insights about people I'm researching. Most of the books I research and write are about plants, gardens, and the natural world, but they are also about politics and people. All are about the relationship between man and nature. For all the joy and excitement that archives hold, nothing really compares to the gardens and landscapes themselves. There is little point in writing about them without having experienced them.

For my book *Founding Gardeners*, I was lucky enough to spend some precious time at Mount Vernon. There, I found myself sitting on Windsor chairs on George Washington's porch overlooking the Potomac, on a boat out on that river to see how the house would often have been approached during his time, in a hot-air balloon above the gardens, and driving around the estate in a garden cart. Those were some of my favorite moments of "research." So many things became clearer when I experienced the landscape of Mount Vernon—seeing, smelling, and feeling the gardens and surroundings that Washington had created.

Washington regarded himself foremost as a farmer and gardener, not as a politician or general. To me, one of the most striking examples of the significance of this is a letter he wrote in the summer of 1776 to his cousin Lund Washington, who served as estate manager at Mount Vernon. America had just declared its independence, George Washington was commander-in-chief, and more than thirty thousand British troops were readying themselves to attack his army in New York. Preoccupied as he doubtless was with devising military strategies and consulting with his officers, on August 19, only two days before the British attacked, he put aside the military maps and wrote to Lund, instructing him to plant two new groves to the north and south of the Mansion. One, the general noted, should be entirely planted with locusts, while for the other he ordered those "clever kind[s] of Trees (especially flowering ones) that can be got."[1]

*Mansion and bowling green from the west, 2014.*

As the chaos of combat and bloodshed loomed, Washington was thinking of crab apple trees, willows, and tulip poplars as well as of flowering dogwoods, mountain laurel, and sassafras. Even more remarkable than the timing of this correspondence was that he specified native species. At a time when other American gardeners were trying to re-create the gardens of the Old World by planting European species, Washington was taking trees and shrubs from his forests and placing them on the grounds of his home. For me, this letter seems like Washington's personal horticultural declaration of independence. At the very moment when the almighty British army threatened to crush the young nation, he evidently decided that no English tree was to root itself in the soil at Mount Vernon.

Years later, when he lived in New York and then Philadelphia during his presidency, he longed to go home to Mount Vernon. With no provisions made in the new U.S. Constitution for a limited number of terms, most Americans assumed Washington would serve for life. But he had other plans. When he retired in 1797, at the end of his second term, in order to return to farming and gardening, he gave the United States the concept of the two-term presidency. It's almost as if one of the enduring tenets of the American presidency stemmed from Washington's passion for his gardens and fields.

Even his death was strangely garden-related. On December 12, 1799, as hail, rain, and snow whipped around Mount Vernon, Washington rode for hours across the estate to inspect his farms. The next day, he felt ill but was determined to mark some trees on the east lawn "to be cut down in the improvement of that spot."[2] He awoke that night, shivering and feverish, and doctors were summoned. But once they had completed their treatment of bleeding and purging, their patient was so weakened that nothing more could be done. Washington died what might be called a gardener's death on December 14.

*The General in the Garden* brings together a wonderful range of material related to Mount Vernon's landscape. It reveals Washington's ideas and inspirations—from books, friends, and other gardens. It also places him firmly within his gardens and describes how the landscape has changed over time. The book is as much about George Washington the man as about the stewardship of the estate—from its rescue by the Mount Vernon Ladies' Association in 1860 to the up-to-date archaeological methods that have informed recent changes in the upper garden. Most of all, *The General in the Garden* shows that Washington's spirit lives on in the gardens and groves of Mount Vernon.

*Lower garden in 2012, showing terraces.*

# Preface and Acknowledgments

The *General in the Garden: George Washington's Landscape at Mount Vernon* presents three intertwined stories. The first is the story of a place: the memorable landscape that surrounds Washington's residence. The second is the story of the man who created that place, the man who led American forces to victory in the Revolutionary War and then relinquished power, returning to private life and embracing the role of the American Cincinnatus. The third is a story of historic preservation, of ongoing efforts to present the Mount Vernon landscape as closely as possible to its appearance in 1799, the last year of George Washington's life.

Located on a high bluff with a commanding view of the Potomac River, about fifteen miles south of Washington, D.C., Mount Vernon is truly a special place. Even when crowded with tourists, the landscape enchants and inspires. Rounding the corner of the Mansion to gaze out over the river or walking beneath one of the tulip poplar trees that Washington planted, it is easy to feel transported back in time, to imagine standing with him at the creation of America.

"No estate in United America is more pleasantly situated than this," Washington asserted in 1793, and few visitors would disagree. Dozens of paintings and prints and countless photographs testify to Mount Vernon's picture-perfect beauty, understood in the eighteenth century as "picturesque." Adapting the precepts of English naturalistic gardening to the local terrain and climate, Washington skillfully reworked nature to create seemingly natural scenes. He had earth moved, leveling the surface west of the Mansion to make the bowling green and sculpting the eastern slope to enhance the view of the Potomac. He ordered gravel hauled up from the riverbank to cover garden pathways, and he marked trees to be transplanted from forests in the outlying sectors of his property. He sought plants and seeds from throughout the American states and from as far abroad as the West Indies, England, and even China.

*Mansion, carriage circle, and several outbuildings, 2007.*

The present book grew from research conducted for a 2014–16 exhibition in the F. M. Kirby Foundation Gallery of Mount Vernon's Donald W. Reynolds Museum and Education Center.

Entitled *Gardens & Groves: George Washington's Landscape at Mount Vernon*, the installation presented a selection of period views, manuscripts, books, artifacts, and archaeological finds aimed at helping visitors better understand and appreciate the historic landscape. Remarkably, this was the first major museum exhibition to focus specifically on Washington's landmark achievements as a landscape designer.

As the project evolved, we realized that understanding Mount Vernon's grounds offered a fruitful means of understanding George Washington himself. From his youthful experiences as a backcountry surveyor to his acquisition and display of paintings representing American scenery to his efforts to reform American agriculture, his love of nature and the land comprised one of the most prominent passions of Washington's life. When he went back to private life at the end of the Revolutionary War, he echoed and embraced the exemplary virtues of the ancient Roman general Cincinnatus, who had left his farm to organize an army and lead it to triumph, then gave up his title to return to his land. The general in the garden is thus the flesh-and-blood counterpart of the idealized hero celebrated in so many statues and paintings. Investigating Washington in this setting and this role vividly links the public leader to the private citizen, thereby illuminating his indispensable role in the winning of independence and his prescient vision for the nation's future.

Two centuries after George Washington and his cadre of gardeners and laborers—hired and enslaved—installed Mount Vernon's landscape, the site retains a rich array of surviving features, including numerous eighteenth-century service buildings. When the Mount Vernon Ladies' Association of the Union acquired 200 acres of the estate in 1860, the group's founder, Ann Pamela Cunningham, rejected sentiments that the outbuildings were of no consequence and should be demolished. Thanks to her inclusive vision for preservation, Mount Vernon escaped the fate of so many historic houses, marooned amid alien surroundings. Since the mid-twentieth century, stewardship of the estate has extended beyond its physical boundaries to encompass Washington's visual landscape, with the Ladies' Association partnering with conservation groups and private landowners to prevent unsightly encroachments on the remarkable vista across the Potomac. Efforts to preserve that vista established important precedents for America's historic preservation movement, especially the value of setting as a key characteristic in assessing the significance of a given property.

It has been my great pleasure and privilege to lead the collaborative four-year effort that has culminated in this publication. Three of my Mount Vernon colleagues have contributed essays offering complementary perspectives on Washington's gardens and grounds. In "Designing the Beautiful: General Washington's Landscape Improvements, 1784–1787," assistant curator Adam T. Erby focuses attention on the relatively brief period during which the recently retired General Washington poured his intense energies into creating a "pleasure ground," using art and artifice creatively to enhance the natural beauty of Mount Vernon's site. In "George Washington's Gardens: Under the Watchful Eye of the Mount Vernon Ladies," J. Dean Norton draws upon his unique experience as the estate's director of horticulture to trace the changing contours of the landscape since 1860.

Finally, in "'Laid out in squares, and boxed with great precission': Uncovering George Washington's Upper Garden," archaeologist Esther C. White describes the extensive fieldwork that uncovered—for the first time—clear physical evidence of the paths and planting beds of Washington's more ornamental garden. Following the essays, Adam Erby's "Gardens and Groves: A Landscape Guide" presents a descriptive catalogue, effectively "decoding" the overall design by focusing attention on its individual components. Lists of documented plants, trees, shrubs, and vines that were planted at Mount Vernon in Washington's day conclude the main text.

Numerous colleagues provided this project with invaluable assistance. Mary V. Thompson and Eleanor Breen shared their extensive knowledge of documentary and archaeological resources, respectively. Michele Lee guided us to the most relevant rare books and manuscripts. Eric Benson and Luke Pecoraro located and mapped landscape features. Kristin Prommel assisted in compiling the list of trees, shrubs, and vines. Dawn M. Bonner located images, managed digital resources, and confirmed permissions requests. Stephen A. McLeod expertly guided the book from manuscript to finished volume, with much appreciated assistance from Michael Kane.

We are most grateful to author Andrea Wulf, whose lively writings on America's founding gardeners have sparked widespread interest in the importance of horticulture to the nation's early leaders, for her thoughtful and generous foreword to this book. Joel T. Fry, curator at Bartram's Garden in Philadelphia, helped us understand Washington's 1792 plant lists. Chris Kolbe, of the Library of Virginia, Richmond, facilitated photography of an early drawing of Mount Vernon's greenhouse. National Park Service bureau historian John H. Sprinkle, Jr., generously shared his research on the preservation of Washington's view across the Potomac. John Henley produced stunning landscape photography, displaying Mount Vernon's grounds to best effect through the seasons. Jeff Glotze and Karen Price assisted with photography. Additional photography came from Robert Shenk and Sarah C. Wolfe, who also designed the exhibition and contributed her skills to the preliminary planning for this book. Manuscript editor Phil Freshman effected a stronger and more readable text, pushing each author to restructure sentences and clarify ideas. Monica S. Rumsey constructed the indexes. Designer Julia Sedykh transformed our words and images into a book that is graceful, appealing, and substantive; we are most appreciative of both her skills and her responsiveness.

For their support of this project, we thank Curtis G. Viebranz, Mount Vernon's president and CEO; Carol Borchert Cadou, senior vice president for historic preservation and collections; and the chairs of the collections and preservation committees, Mrs. P. Coleman Townsend, Jr., and Mrs. Frank Mauran IV. Douglas Bradburn, founding director of the Fred W. Smith National Library for the Study of George Washington, embraced *The General in the Garden* as the first publication project carried out under the Library's auspices, initiating a collaboration with the University of Virginia Press. Susan Magill, vice president for advancement, and F. Anderson Morse, director of development, enthusiastically championed the project to interested supporters.

Publication of *The General in the Garden* was underwritten by generous contributions from the

Nimick Forbesway Foundation, The Life Guard Society of Historic Mount Vernon, and the David Bruce Smith Book Fund. We are also grateful for additional contributions that supported the exhibition, from The Life Guard Society of Historic Mount Vernon, the Dr. Scholl Foundation, the Nimick Forbesway Foundation, the Stella Boyle Smith Trust, the Neighborhood Friends of Mount Vernon, and an anonymous donor.

Distinguished by its beauty, its historical associations, its level of preservation, and its extensive archival and archaeological record, George Washington's landscape at Mount Vernon is by any standard a true national treasure, of incomparable value not only for its own sake but also as a window onto the larger American cultural landscape. I invite you to dip into the pages that follow, and also to visit Mount Vernon to walk the paths and savor the views that Washington planned and brought to life so long ago.

SUSAN P. SCHOELWER
*Robert H. Smith Senior Curator*
*George Washington's Mount Vernon*

RIGHT: *Formal boxwood parterre in upper garden, 2014.* OVERLEAF: *John Trumbull, George Washington at Verplanck's Point, 1790 (detail).*

# The General in the Garden

# DESIGNING THE BEAUTIFUL

## General Washington's Landscape Improvements, 1784–1787

### Adam T. Erby

*"In a word the garden, the plantations, the house, the whole upkeep, proves that a man born with natural taste can divine the beautiful without having seen the model. The [General] has never left America. After seeing his house and his gardens one would say that he had seen the most beautiful examples in England."*

Julian Ursyn Niemcewicz, 1798

*Samuel Vaughan's 1787 sketch and presentation drawing of the Mount Vernon landscape.*

With these effusive words of praise, the Polish nobleman Julian Ursyn Niemcewicz recorded his impressions of George Washington's estate one year after the general retired from the presidency and finally returned to his beloved Mount Vernon.[1] Like generations of visitors who have flocked to the home of the father of American independence, Niemcewicz was moved by the natural beauty of the place and by the seamless integration of the natural world and the built environment. He recognized that Mount Vernon's beauty was no mere accident but rather the result of careful design and thoughtful planning by the master of the estate. George Washington developed the landscape that Niemcewicz so admired primarily in the few short years between the conclusion of the Revolutionary War and the beginning of the Constitutional Convention. During this period, he dedicated the year 1784 to designing the landscape and then implemented his plan between 1785 and 1787. By the time he left for Philadelphia in the spring of 1787, he had only minor adjustments to make—the outline had been laid and the plants were beginning to grow. It is this landscape, created during Washington's relatively brief respite from public duties, that Mount Vernon continues to preserve to this day.[2]

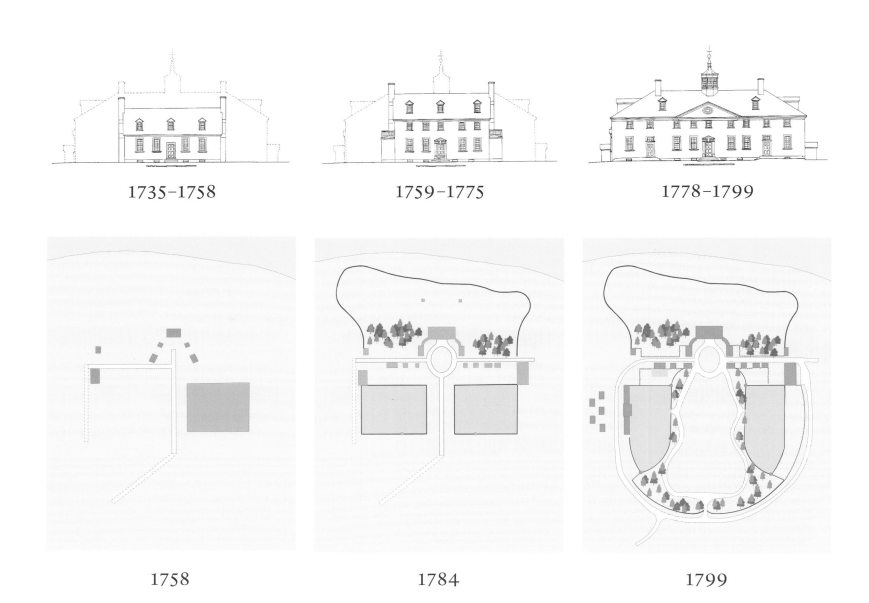

1735–1758

1759–1775

1778–1799

1758

1784

1799

## The Early Years at Mount Vernon

When George Washington took a lifetime lease on Mount Vernon from the widow of his elder half-brother, Lawrence, in 1754, the estate had an entirely different look and feel. At that time, the house was a much smaller dwelling—large for the time but small in comparison to the Mansion it would become. The kitchen, dairy, and other outbuildings were arranged in a symmetrical pattern that radiated from the house, emphasizing its architectural massing and lending a genteel feeling to the estate. These outbuildings provided the services needed by the Washington family, and little effort was made to mask the messy processes that each contained. Farther away from the house, a small kitchen garden provided the fruits and vegetables needed by the household, but there were no formal gardens like those found on the impressive Tidewater estates of the Carters, the Byrds, the Randolphs, and other leading Virginia families. Rather, the grounds surrounding the early house at Mount Vernon were laid out more for efficiency than for pleasure.[3]

Over the succeeding decades, Washington made incremental changes to both the Mansion and landscape. In the spring of 1757, he began expanding the house by adding a full second story and garret, as he prepared to find a wife, settle down, and start a family. In January 1759, shortly before the completion of this expansion, Washington married the wealthy widow Martha Dandridge Custis. That same year, he wrote his London purchasing agent for a copy of Batty Langley's influential book *New Principles of Gardening* (1728), presumably with the intention of overhauling the design of Mount Vernon's landscape and installing pleasure grounds for the enjoyment of his family and guests.[4] Although Langley designed very few gardens and was not a major leader of Britain's landscape design movement, his was one of the earliest books written on naturalistic gardening. He successfully distilled his own ideas together with those of the great lights, such as the famous architect William Kent, into a heavily illustrated publication that was well received in the American colonies. Langley provided instructions for building an elaborated landscape garden, or pleasure ground, along with a variety of inset plates with sample designs for his readers.[5]

Approaches to landscape design in Britain evolved over the course of the eighteenth century, from the formal clipped hedges, radiating walks, and contrived geometry of an earlier era to more natural compositions. Batty Langley's designs fell somewhere between the two extremes of the formal and the naturalistic. While his text offered practical suggestions for creating more naturalistic gardens—by including good shade, uninterrupted views, and frequent "irregularities," thus avoiding stiffness and tiresome repetition—the accompanying illustrations presented a contradictory maze of parterres and angular lines harking back to formal French gardens of the seventeenth century.[6]

Proponents of the shift toward naturalism emphasized the use of curved lines to give a more organic appearance to landscape design. British landscape architects were inspired by the paintings of the seventeenth-century French artist Claude Lorrain, and they replicated his dramatic style by

*Evolution of Mansion and surrounding landscape during George Washington's lifetime.*

ABOVE: *South work lane, seen from Mansion cupola, 2012.* RIGHT: *Covered walkway between Mansion and kitchen, 2014.*

framing distant prospects with trees and landscape elements in the foreground. Landscape theorists believed that landscape design should simply improve the beauty already provided by nature.[7]

George Washington demonstrated a clear interest in picturesque landscapes early in life, ordering "A Neat Landskip" after Claude to install in the Mansion's west parlor in 1757.[8] This canvas, created by an unknown artist, depicts several ships on a river framed by a naturalistic image of trees on the banks in the foreground. Additionally, in his first known portrait, painted in 1772 by the American artist Charles Willson Peale, Washington appears as a Virginia militia colonel, with a wild, naturalistic mountain scene in the background. The setting emphasizes his early identification with the wildernesses of western Virginia, Pennsylvania, and the Ohio country, and represents a distinct departure from the Virginia gentry tradition of depicting the sitter's own formal gardens in the backgrounds of portraits.[9] Washington continued to collect landscape art for the rest of his life, purchasing large paintings depicting the courses of American rivers during his two terms as president and buying prints after oils by Claude for display at Mount Vernon. These scenes testify to Washington's interest in the natural landscape and his desire to open up the grounds around Mount Vernon to highlight the natural beauty of the place.[10]

## Expansion before the Revolutionary War

Washington's acquisition of Batty Langley's book in 1759 suggests that he may have been planning a major overhaul of the Mount Vernon landscape; however, other, more pressing concerns intervened. In the early years after his 1759 marriage, Washington concentrated his attention on becoming a successful planter and providing for his new family. He did not return to the landscape project until the mid-1770s, just before the outbreak of the Revolutionary War, when he radically altered the Mansion, the surrounding outbuildings, and the gardens to the west of the house.

He began by adding two wings to the Mansion—a study and master bedchamber to the south, balanced by a large entertaining space to the north. Initially, these wings were partly blocked from view by the outbuildings radiating from the Mansion, so Washington removed the older structures he had inherited from his brother and replaced them with newer buildings in a more harmonious design. On either side of the carriage circle on the west side of the Mansion, he added identical, one-and-a-half-story outbuildings to balance the house and enhance its Georgian symmetry. The building to the south served as a kitchen, while the one to the north served a variety of functions, including lodging for the white servants of Washington's guests. He also added a pair of arcaded walkways, which connected the outbuildings to the Mansion both visually and physically, the one linking the kitchen offering a covered passage for enslaved servants delivering meals to the house.[11]

When Washington replaced the remaining outbuildings, he located them on two lanes running perpendicular to the central carriage lane. The strategic placement of these buildings allowed the kitchen and white-servants' hall to block the view toward the other buildings from the Mansion,

*George Washington installed this "Neat Landskip" (after Claude Lorrain) in the Mansion's west parlor in 1757.*

LEFT: *George Beck*, The Great Falls of the Potomac River, *circa 1797.* ABOVE: *Charles Willson Peale,* George Washington as a Colonel in the Virginia Regiment, *1772.*

thus concealing such messy processes as butchering and smoking meat, laundering clothes, and other chores. At the same time, he enclosed the upper garden with a rectangular brick wall, mirroring the wall that surrounded the lower garden, which had been added some years earlier. The addition of the final brick wall effectively cut off the view to the west of the Mansion and channeled visitors' paths along the carriage way between the exterior brick walls of the two gardens.

But this iteration of the Mount Vernon landscape was not yet complete, and George Washington assumed command of the Continental Army in June 1775, before he could finish the work. A year later, during the siege of New York, as the general waited for a British attack on his troops, he wrote a remarkably detailed letter to his cousin Lund Washington, who managed Mount Vernon in his absence, instructing him to plant groves of trees to the north and south of the Mansion. These trees would further block the view of the outbuildings from the house and the east lawn. To the north, Washington wanted a grove consisting entirely of black locusts, but to the south he asked that Lund plant "all the clever kind of Trees (especially flowering ones) that can be got, such as Crab apple, Poplar, Dogwood, Sasafras, Lawrel, Willow (especially yellow & Weeping Willow, twigs of which may be got from Philadelphia)." These he wished to be interspersed with evergreens and "Wild flowering shrubs of the larger kind, such as the fringe tree." In each grove, he directed, the trees were to be planted in a naturalistic style "without any order or regularity."[12] With the plan for these two groves, Washington completed his early vision for the Mount Vernon landscape. It would be eight years before he returned to landscape design.

## A New Plan for Mount Vernon

When Washington came back to Mount Vernon after the Revolutionary War, he found the estate in need of extensive repairs and improvements. During the eight years he had been away leading his troops, he seems to have developed a completely different vision for the gardens and grounds surrounding the Mansion. He recognized that Mount Vernon's position at the crest of a hill overlooking the Potomac River offered enormous aesthetic potential that had not previously been tapped. The general later wrote that "No estate in United America is more pleasantly situated than this," and beginning in 1784, he set out to remake the landscape to take better advantage of its natural features.[13] In redesigning the grounds, he concluded that his earlier design had prevented a full appreciation of the natural beauty of the site. To the west of the Mansion, the view was marred by the two brick-walled gardens he had installed just before he left home in 1775. To the east, the view to the Potomac was interrupted by two "necessaries," outhouses for the Washington family and guests.[14]

Washington's new design for Mount Vernon focused on creating "pleasure grounds," or ornamental gardens, for the enjoyment of his family and guests. This aim represented a radical departure from the purely functional gardens that he had completed immediately before the war. As the central element of the new design, Washington planned to install a broad expanse of grass, or

*Benjamin Henry Latrobe,* View of Mount Vernon Looking to the North, *1796.*

View of Mount Vernon looking to the North July 17th 1796. The portico faces to the East.

*Southeast corner of east lawn, where*
*a "necessary" stood until 1796.*

bowling green, to the west of the Mansion, an element that would have no practical purpose other than providing a beautiful lawn for his guests to enjoy. He intended to edge the bowling green with a serpentine path to guide visitors as they meandered among the trees and flowering shrubs that he planned to plant on either side of the lawn.

The installation of this bowling green required that Washington open up space by demolishing portions of the earlier, brick-walled gardens blocking the view from the Mansion to the west. He replaced these rectangular plots with bullet-shaped gardens on either side of the bowling green, thus accommodating the flaring curves at its widest point. The south, or lower, garden was entirely dedicated to food production and received the best direct sunlight on its two terraces set into the side of a hill. Its brick walls protected the plantings from wildlife and also retained heat, creating a warmer microclimate that extended the growing season for delicate plants. The north, or upper, garden was the more ornamental of the two, and it was intended to be a highlight of a walk through the pleasure grounds. As the centerpiece of the upper garden, Washington intended to construct a large brick greenhouse for the cultivation and display of exotic plants.

Working with far fewer acres than English country estates, however, Washington lacked the option of completely separating the pleasure grounds from the working parts of his plantation. Ever practical, he incorporated rows of vegetables, fruits, and berries into the center of the planting beds of his ornamental flower garden. He bordered the beds with a wide swath of flowering plants, edged by a row of diminutive boxwood. He also cleverly arranged walls, groves, and shrubberies to keep the stable, laundry, blacksmith shop, and slave quarter hidden from the view of the Mansion and pleasure grounds. Such details reveal George Washington's personal involvement and innovation; he drew ideas from English sources but adapted them to suit his own tastes and circumstances. To update Mount Vernon in the new, naturalistic fashion, he installed such stylish features as sweeping lawns, curving paths, groves of trees, wildernesses, vistas, and hidden ha-ha walls (walled ditches that kept livestock from entering the manicured lawn). At the same time, he also retained some stylistically earlier design features, including a symmetrical arrangement of the trees and shrubberies planted on either side of the bowling green and a formal geometric plan within his ornamental flower garden.

Washington had developed a thorough knowledge of Mount Vernon's topography through the countless surveys he made of his land. This intimate understanding enabled him to highlight the natural advantages provided by the rolling hills and to calculate possible sightlines through the woods. The challenges of laying out such a precisely calculated scheme suggest that he may well have used his finely honed surveying skills to create a working drawing that guided his efforts. While no such drawing by Washington for the pleasure grounds is presently known, one seems to have been included in the collection of a Washington descendant in the mid-nineteenth century, recorded by the antiquarian Benson J. Lossing. As reproduced by Lossing in his 1859 publication, *Mount Vernon and Its Associations: Historical, Biographical, and Pictorial*, this drawing resembles Washington's sur-

*Aerial view of Mount Vernon landscape, 2012.*

veys, with each building and landscape feature identified by a letter and explained in a corresponding key.[15]

Lossing's engraving features letters on either side of the serpentine path that seem to correspond with those on a list of trees in George Washington's hand. Each letter represents a specific type of tree on his list—for example, A for fringe trees and B for sassafras.[16] The drawing shows that Washington carefully thought out the placement of each tree and shrub he intended to plant along the bowling green, with an eye toward the overall effect of the composition. Notably, he designed these plantings as mirror images on either side of the green, thus introducing symmetry within the naturalistic contours of the landscape. Rather than wholeheartedly embrace the fully formed naturalism of the British picturesque, Washington chose elements that appealed to him and selectively slotted them into his own design, adapting them to fit his own circumstances.

Like his land surveys, George Washington's landscape design imposed manmade order on the natural world, dividing land into discrete plots. When the Mount Vernon landscape is viewed from above, the layout appears almost completely symmetrical. Buildings are aligned on either side of the carriage circle, the curves of the bowling green and serpentine walk are balanced, and two bullet-shaped gardens border the composition.

This artful landscape design overlay another, less easily visible division of spaces, between two separate but intersecting zones: the pleasure grounds of the elite white planter and the working landscape of the enslaved community. Washington maintained strict boundaries between these two zones, highlighting the hierarchical social order of a Virginia plantation and emphasizing his own authority over the domestic landscape. The bowling green, for example, was reserved for the exclusive use of the family and their guests, and Washington once directed that enslaved children be kept out of the area, as they "too frequently are breaking limbs or twigs from or doing other injury to my shrubs some of which at a considerable expense, have been propagated."[17]

RIGHT: *Spyglass owned by George Washington.*
OPPOSITE: *Benson Lossing's copy of a list of trees (in Washington's hand) and a diagram of trees along the bowling green, both published in 1859.*

a Tulep tree _ _ _ _ _ _ _ _ _ _ _ _ _ 16
b Sassafras _ _ _ _ _ _ _ _ _ _ _ 28
c Papau _ _ _ _ _ _ _ _ _ _ _ 16
d Red Haw _ _ _ _ _ _ _ _ _ 16
e Red bud _ _ _ _ _ _ _ _ _ 32
a Mock Orange _ _ _ _ _ _ _ 2
f Hemlock _ _ _ _ _ _ _ _ _ 28
g Tree at H. hole _ _ _ _ _ 4
g Yellow Willow _ _ _ _ _ 28
h Magnolia _ _ _ _ _ _ _ 28
4 Catalpa _ _ _ _ _ _ _ 4
i Coral tree _ _ _ _ _ _ 28
k Black Haw _ _ _ _ _ _ 16
.x English Walnut _ _ _ _ _ 4
l Holly _ _ _ _ _ _ _ _ _ _ 24
m Lilac _ _ _ _ _ _ _ _ 20
n Dogwood _ _ _ _ _ _ _ 28
o Locust _ _ _ _ _ _ _ _ 28
o Swamp Red berry _ _ _ _ 16
Q Althea _ _ _ _ _ _ _ 16
h Great thorn _ _ _ _ _ 16
r Cedar _ _ _ _ _ _ _ _ 28
S Service _ _ _ _ _ _ _ 6
w Lilac
t Holly & Ivy - above _ _ _

1 Balm of Gil.d or Holly _ _ _
2 Horse Chesnut _ _ _ _ _ 4
3 Lime _ _ _ _ _ _ _ 4
5 Pine _ _ _ _ _ _ _ 20
6 Poplar _ _ _ _ _ _ 20
7 Black Gum _ _ _ _ _ 18
8 Elm _ _ _ _ _ _ 14
9 Maple _ _ _ _ _ _ 22
10 Mulberry _ _ _ _ _ 20
11 Aspan _ _ _ _ _ 20
12 Ash _ _ _ _ _ _ 22
                              596

FAC-SIMILE OF WASHINGTON'S MEMORANDUM.

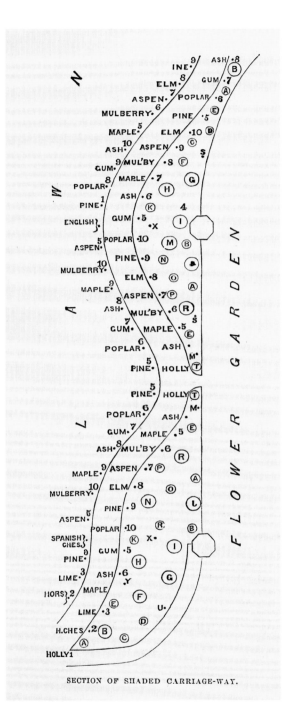

SECTION OF SHADED CARRIAGE-WAY.

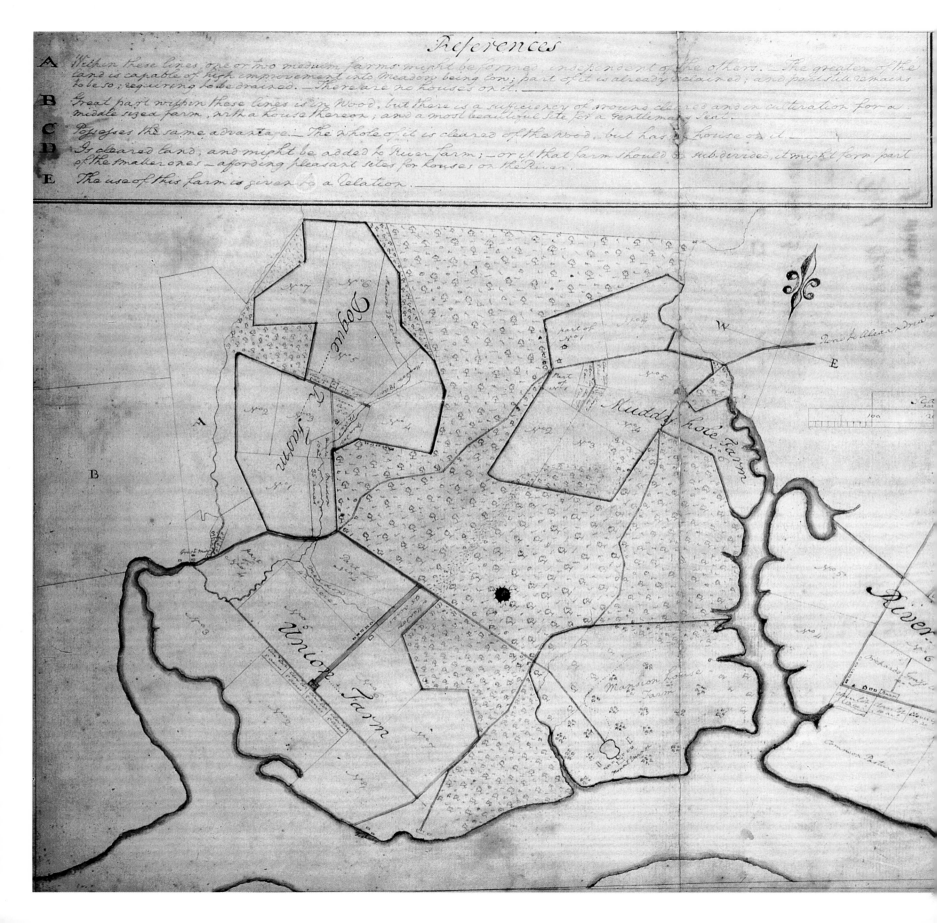

References

A  Within these lines, one or two medium farms might be formed independent of the others. — The greater of the land is capable of high improvement into Meadow being low; part of it is already declared; and part still remains to be so; requiring to be drained. — There are no houses on it.

B  Great part within these lines is in Wood; but there is a sufficiency of ground cleared and in cultivation for a middle sized farm, with a house thereon; and a most beautiful Site for a Gentleman's Seat.

C  Possesses the same advantage. — The whole of it is cleared of the Wood, but has no house on it.

D  Is cleared land, and might be added to River farm; — or if that farm should be subdivided, it might form part of the smaller ones — affording pleasant sites for houses on the River.

E  The use of this farm is given to a relation.

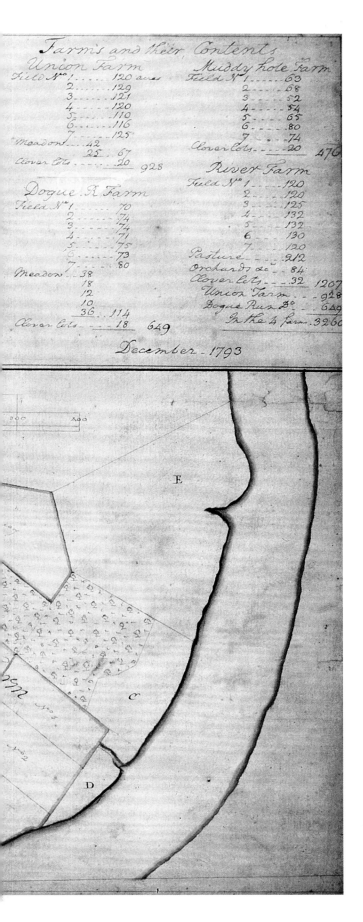

Farms and their Contents

Union Farm
Field Nᵒ 1 ..... 120 acres
2 ..... 129
3 ..... 121
4 ..... 120
5 ..... 110
6 ..... 116
7 ..... 125
Meadow ... 42
25 . 67
Clover &ᶜ ... 20    928

Dogue R. Farm
Field Nᵒ 1 ..... 70
2 ..... 74
3 ..... 74
4 ..... 71
5 ..... 75
6 ..... 73
7 ..... 80
Meadow ... 38
18
12
10
36 .. 114
Clover &ᶜ ... 18    649

Muddy hole Farm
Field Nᵒ 1 ..... 63
2 ..... 68
3 ..... 52
4 ..... 54
5 ..... 65
6 ..... 80
7 ..... 74
Clover &ᶜ ... 20    476

River Farm
Field Nᵒ 1 ..... 120
2 ..... 120
3 ..... 125
4 ..... 132
5 ..... 132
6 ..... 130
7 ..... 120
Pasture ... 212
Orchards &ᶜ ... 84
Clover &ᶜ ... 32    1207
Union Farm ... 928
Dogue Run &ᶜ ... 649
In the 4 Farm. 3260

December . 1793

E

C

D

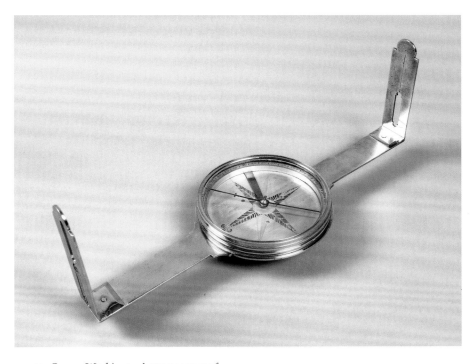

LEFT: *George Washington's 1793 survey of Mount Vernon's five farms.* ABOVE: *Washington's surveyor's compass, which he may have used to determine boundaries for his surveys and to lay out straight lines in his gardens.*

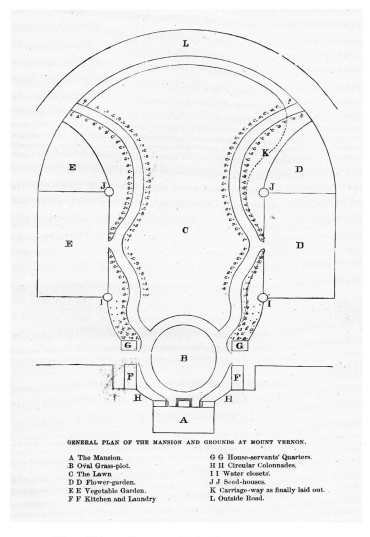

GENERAL PLAN OF THE MANSION AND GROUNDS AT MOUNT VERNON.

| | |
|---|---|
| A The Mansion. | G G House-servants' Quarters. |
| B Oval Grass-plot. | H H Circular Colonnades. |
| C The Lawn | I I Water closets. |
| D D Flower-garden. | J J Seed-houses. |
| E E Vegetable Garden. | K Carriage-way as finally laid out. |
| F F Kitchen and Laundry | L Outside Road. |

ABOVE: *Plan of Mount Vernon, published by Benson Lossing in 1859.* RIGHT: *Serpentine path, spring 2012.*

# George Washington's Design Sources

Although scholars have often attempted to link Washington's design for the pleasure grounds at Mount Vernon to specific design sources, such efforts fail to convey the complexity of his plan and the intense involvement of the man himself.[18] Washington's landscape design is an original composition expressing his own aesthetic, developed from deep familiarity with plants and trees, a love for and appreciation of the land, and his own experience as a surveyor. As he designed Mount Vernon's pleasure grounds between 1784 and 1785, he drew inspiration from English books and the finest gardens of the American elite. He adopted these ideas selectively in a way that suited the needs of his Virginia plantation and took full advantage of the site itself.

Like Batty Langley's *New Principles of Gardening*, the vast majority of gardening manuals and design books imported to America were written by British authors and provided advice specific to the growing conditions and landed estates found in Great Britain. Notably, Washington adapted this advice to an American context, where gardens were smaller and more compact. He also maintained an experimental garden, where he could test the growing methods recommended in the garden manuals and determine appropriate techniques for Virginia soil and climate. Washington seems to have learned the most from Philip Miller's influential *Gardener's Dictionary*, which was initially published in 1731 and purchased by Washington in its abridged version in 1763. It contained an extensive list of plants with instructions for their cultivation. Washington relied upon this book in planting his kitchen garden, and several memoranda survive with his handwritten notes on transplanting various trees, copied directly from Miller.[19]

Wherever George Washington traveled, he visited the homes of local gentry, displaying a keen interest in their gardens. He determined what he liked or did not like about a particular estate and recorded these observations in his journal. In 1787, after touring the famous nursery that had been established by the botanist John Bartram outside Philadelphia, Washington observed that although the garden was "Stored with many curious pl[an]ts. Shrubs & trees, many of which are exotics [, it] was not laid off with much taste, nor was it large."[20] By contrast, he was so impressed with the greenhouse at Mount Clare, Margaret Tilghman Carroll's home outside Baltimore, that he based elements of his own greenhouse on hers.[21]

Beyond consulting garden-design books and observing the efforts of American gardeners, Washington drew inspiration from the natural wonders of America's landscapes. As early as 1748, when traveling west to survey for the Fairfax family, he had admired the grand drama created by scenes viewed from high prospects, such as mountains. In the Shenandoah Valley, he recorded that "higher up the River we went through most beautiful Groves of Sugar Trees & spent the best part of the Day in admiring the Trees & richness of the Land."[22] He would later use this experience to advantage when clearing the view to the Potomac River and the vistas west of the Mansion.

TOP LEFT: *Charles Willson Peale's 1770–71 portrait of Margaret Tilghman Carroll in her garden, holding an orange branch from her greenhouse.*
BOTTOM LEFT: *John Bartram's house and gardens, outside Philadelphia.*
RIGHT: *Washington's copy of Batty Langley's* New Principles of Gardening *(1728).*

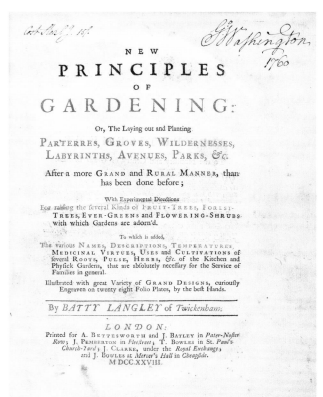

On the cold morning of January 12, 1785, George Washington set out on horseback after breakfast to make the rounds to each of his five farms. When at Mount Vernon, he made this same circuit almost daily to inspect the fields or to check on the progress of improvements to the estate. But that January morning, Washington rode out with a very different purpose in mind; he was searching his forests to find "the sort of Trees I shall want for my Walks, groves, and Wildernesses."[23] Mount Vernon's many forested acres served as the nursery that would furnish the rich variety of trees he wished to plant along the serpentine path edging the bowling green.

It is no coincidence that during the first six months of Washington's major landscape overhaul, from January to June 1785, the activity recorded most frequently in his diary is the planting and transplanting of trees. He had spent much of his life exploring the woods, first as a surveyor recording the vast landholdings of the Fairfax family across the Blue Ridge Mountains and later as a frontier military officer. This extensive travel through the American landscape brought Washington face to face with the soaring majesty of tulip poplars, the soft pink and white blossoms of dogwoods in the spring, and the vibrant reds and oranges of maples in the fall. His firsthand knowledge of nature allowed him to identify the types of trees he wanted, even in the depths of winter, by the color and texture of the bark on their leafless limbs and their overall shape.

Upon returning home in 1785 from each day's journey into the woods, Washington recorded the types of trees he had found and where he had found them. At the site of his gristmill, he found "some young Crab apple trees and young Pine trees in the old field of all sizes."[24] When the crab apple bloomed each spring, its thick canopy was covered with vibrant red flowers, providing a burst of color to the landscape.

By January 19, 1785, Washington and his enslaved workers had begun laying out the "serpentine road" that would define the outline of the guitar-shaped bowling green just west of the Mansion. His design for the serpentine path was precisely calculated to fit with the other major elements of the landscape, so he supervised the work himself. Later in the month, the arrival of several visitors interrupted his progress and pushed completion back a few days, but by the end of January, the path had been entirely laid out. The slaves then began the arduous task of carting pebbles dredged from the Potomac River up the hillside to gravel the path's surface. Over the next several weeks, Washington carefully oversaw the transplanting of flowering shrubs and trees along the edges of the bowling green.[25]

As Washington continued to transplant trees from his own plantation, he began receiving specimens of additional varieties not native to Virginia. From a nephew in South Carolina, he requested seed of the "Ever-green Magnolia—this latter is called in Millers Gardeners dictionary greater Magnolia—it rises according to his Acc[oun]t to the height of Eighty feet or more—flowers early, & is a beautiful tree" and also a few seeds of the live oak tree.[26] He also wrote to Governor George

*One of the tulip poplar trees George Washington planted in 1785.*

Clinton of New York, seeking the evergreen "Balm tree, White & Spruce pine" for his pine labyrinths at the western end of the bowling green.[27]

The major problem with transplanting young trees in the middle of the winter is that they are vulnerable to the weight of ice and snow in their new locations when not protected by other, taller trees and plants beside them. Calamity struck Mount Vernon on the night of March 8, 1785, when Washington recorded seeing "the heaviest rain I ever recollect." The next morning, the ground was covered with two inches of snow, and "the bows of all the trees were encrusted by tubes of Ice, at least half an Inch thick." The condition of the many freshly planted trees was not very good, and the weight of the ice caused many of the limbs to break and the bodies of the young trees to bow out of shape. Washington was not deterred by the setback, however. Two days later, when the snow and ice had melted, he took up the spade again and was back at work.[28]

Significant work continued throughout the late winter and early spring, and by the middle of April 1785, Washington recorded in his diary that the many small trees he had worked so diligently to plant were beginning to show signs of life: "The buds of every kind of tree and shrub are swelling, the tender leaves of many had unfolded." He was delighted with the variety of color provided by the maple trees he had planted, as there was a "great difference in the colour of the blossoms [buds]; some being of a deep scarlet, bordering upon crimson, others of a pale red, approaching yellow."[29] But Washington's excitement at the coming of spring was dampened by a late frost and ice storm that left his plants once more covered with ice. Although the plants were sickly, they began to take hold that year. By the time he traveled to Philadelphia in the spring of 1787, most had taken root and were beginning to flourish.[30]

## The Hired Gardeners

As George Washington laid out Mount Vernon's pleasure grounds between 1785 and 1787, he required the labor of both free and enslaved workers. He personally directed the work of the "Mansion house people"—the slaves on the home farm—as they transplanted trees, built brick walls, and graveled the serpentine path. He also worked closely with Philip Bateman, who had been hired in 1773 to oversee the production of fruits and vegetables for use in the kitchen. Very little is known of Bateman's training, but he likely learned his trade in North America and, presumably, had not received the specialized training of a true professional gardener.[31]

With the completion of his greenhouse in 1787, Washington sought to hire a professional gardener with experience raising tropical plants and the ability to operate the complicated subterranean heating system he had installed. Few Americans had experience raising plants in a greenhouse, so he looked to Europe to recruit "a compleat Kitchen Gardener with a competent knowledge of

*Front of greenhouse and rear of slave quarter wings, 2014.*

Flowers and a Green House" to maintain the pleasure grounds and superintend new projects.[32] In the late eighteenth century, Europe had an overabundance of well-educated and highly trained gardeners who had served their apprenticeships on landed estates but found little opportunity to advance their careers or earn higher wages.

In November 1788, Henrich Wilmans of Bremen, Germany, dined at Mount Vernon and offered to engage a gardener for Washington in his native land. The following year, Wilmans hired John Christian Ehlers on Washington's behalf, sending him aboard the *Minerva* to New York, where he was met by the president's personal secretary, Tobias Lear, and was dispatched by stagecoach to Mount Vernon. Ehlers was a professional gardener who had served his apprenticeship in Hanover, Germany, at the royal gardens at Montbrillant, owned by England's King George III. Unfortunately, Ehlers spoke no English when he arrived, and he requested that Washington send an English-Dutch (likely Deutsch, or German) dictionary to help him learn the new language.[33]

The hiring of a trained European gardener for Mount Vernon served as a visible manifestation of George Washington's taste and sophistication, elevating his gardens from ordinary kitchen gardens to spaces to showcase and experiment with rare and exotic plants for the table. In Washington's absence, Ehlers likely provided tours of the pleasure grounds, pointing out plants by their Latin names. He probably displayed at least a rudimentary knowledge of botany, geology, physics, and chemistry—sciences that would have proven useful when conversing with Washington's many educated visitors.[34]

LEFT: *Vegetables in upper garden, 2011.* RIGHT: *Interior of gardener's house, 2013. John Christian Ehlers moved into these rooms in 1793 after his wife, Catherine, arrived from Bremen.*

The German gardener typically oversaw two or three enslaved laborers, including at various times Frank Lee, Harry, Sam, George, and the former cook, Hercules. Enslaved children at the Mansion House Farm performed less onerous tasks, such as raking grass clippings or picking up fallen sticks.[35] Ehlers reported to the farm manager, the highest-ranking hired servant at Mount Vernon, to whom the vast majority of the workers reported. While serving as president, Washington required that both the farm manager and the gardener send reports "to the Post Office every Wednesday."[36] In these reports, the two men listed the tasks accomplished each week and the time spent by each laborer.

Returning from the presidency in 1797, George Washington parted ways with Ehlers, after almost eight years. He had grown weary of Ehlers's inability to "refrain from spiritous liquors" and his propensity toward idleness.[37] Washington then wrote to James Anderson, a friend and economist living in Scotland, requesting assistance in finding a gardener who had apprenticed at one of the aristocratic estates there. The former president sought a Scotsman because he believed that "generally speaking, they are more orderly & industrious, than those of other nations," and the climate in parts of Scotland was similar to that of Virginia. Several months later, Anderson hired William Spence on Washington's behalf and sent him to Mount Vernon, where he would serve as gardener until Washington's death in 1799.[38] Washington was quite satisfied with Spence's work at Mount Vernon. "I never had a hired servant that pleased me better," he wrote to Anderson in 1798, "and what adds to my satisfaction is that he is content himself, having declared he never was happier in his life."[39]

## Samuel Vaughan's Presentation Drawing of 1787

By May 1787, when Washington departed for the Constitutional Convention in Philadelphia, his work on the Mount Vernon landscape was nearly complete, needing only the passing seasons for plantings to become established. That August, while Washington was presiding over the heated debates that shaped the U.S. Constitution, his friend Samuel Vaughan visited Mount Vernon at the end of a sightseeing tour of sites associated with the Revolutionary War. An enthusiastic supporter of the American cause, Vaughan was a wealthy British merchant who had arrived in Philadelphia in September 1783, just days after the signing of the Treaty of Paris formally ended the war. He had long admired General Washington and succeeded in meeting him through the Philadelphia Society for Promoting Agriculture. When the two met, the general was beginning to think about improvements he wished to make at Mount Vernon, and Vaughan provided valuable information on the latest English ideas about both landscape design and interior furnishings. He presented Washington with an elaborate marble mantelpiece, carved with bucolic farming scenes that embodied the two men's idealized vision of rural life. Removed from Vaughan's own country house outside London, the mantelpiece still graces the Mansion's "New Room."[40]

LEFT: *"New Room" mantle, designed by Sir Henry Cheere, England, circa 1770.* RIGHT: *Robert Edge Pine, Samuel Vaughan, 1760.*

During his visit to Mount Vernon, Vaughan explored the estate, took detailed measurements of the Mansion and its immediate surroundings, and made a rough sketch in his small travel journal. He subsequently compiled this information into a large finished drawing, which he presented to the general. Samuel Vaughan's presentation drawing delineates the major elements of George Washington's pleasure grounds, with a lettered key at the lower right that identifies specific landscape features. Seen at the top are the sweeping curves of the Potomac River and the expanse of the east lawn. Groves of trees, planted irregularly, flank the house. The formal geometry of the Mansion carriage circle and the straight lines of outbuildings and garden pathways contrast strongly with the serpentine path that borders the central bowling green. Washington praised Vaughan's accuracy, noting only that the trees came too close to the gate at the west end of the lawn (the bottom of the drawing).[41]

Known today as the "Vaughan plan," this bird's-eye view precisely captures Washington's design for his pleasure grounds. Preserved among his papers after his death, the original drawing descended among family members until it was acquired by Mount Vernon in 1975. Vaughan's drawing provides invaluable documentation about the appearance of the estate in Washington's day, guiding the restoration of landscape elements that have disappeared over time.

## A Symbolic Addition to Mount Vernon

During the brief period between the end of the Revolutionary War and the Constitutional Convention, George Washington had finally been able to complete his design for both his home and his landscape, in anticipation of what he hoped would be a long and happy retirement. In the summer of 1787, he added a finishing touch to the Mansion, installing at the center of the roof a hexagonal cupola with six windows. In addition to supplying a means of venting the summer heat, the cupola provided a vertical element to the strongly horizontal massing of the house.

In Philadelphia, Washington wrote to house carpenter Joseph Rakestraw, asking the craftsman to create a weathervane to place atop the cupola: "I should like to have a bird (in place of the Vain)," Washington instructed, "with an olive branch in its Mouth—the bird need not be large (for I do not expect traverse with the wind and therefore may receive the real shape of a bird, with spread wings."[42] The weathervane Rakestraw provided took the form of a gilded dove with a black-painted beak holding a green olive branch, evoking the ancient Greek and biblical symbol for peace. The installation of the weathervane provided a fitting conclusion to Washington's landscape design, reminding his guests that, at the end of the Revolutionary War, the general who had led the American army returned home in peace to concentrate on improving his estate rather than taking the reins of power.[43]

*Mansion cupola, topped by replica of Washington's original dove of peace weathervane, 2013.*

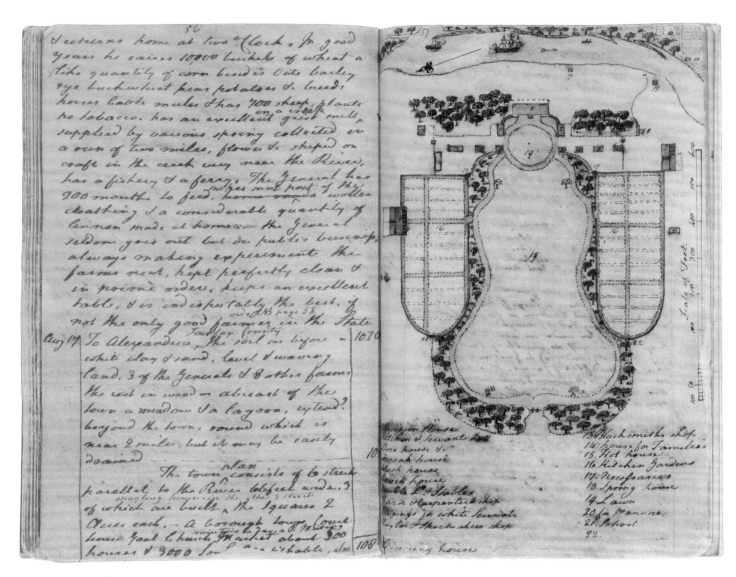

ABOVE: *Samuel Vaughan's 1787 journal, with sketch of the Mount Vernon landscape.* RIGHT, PAGE 37: *Vaughan's 1787 presentation drawing.*

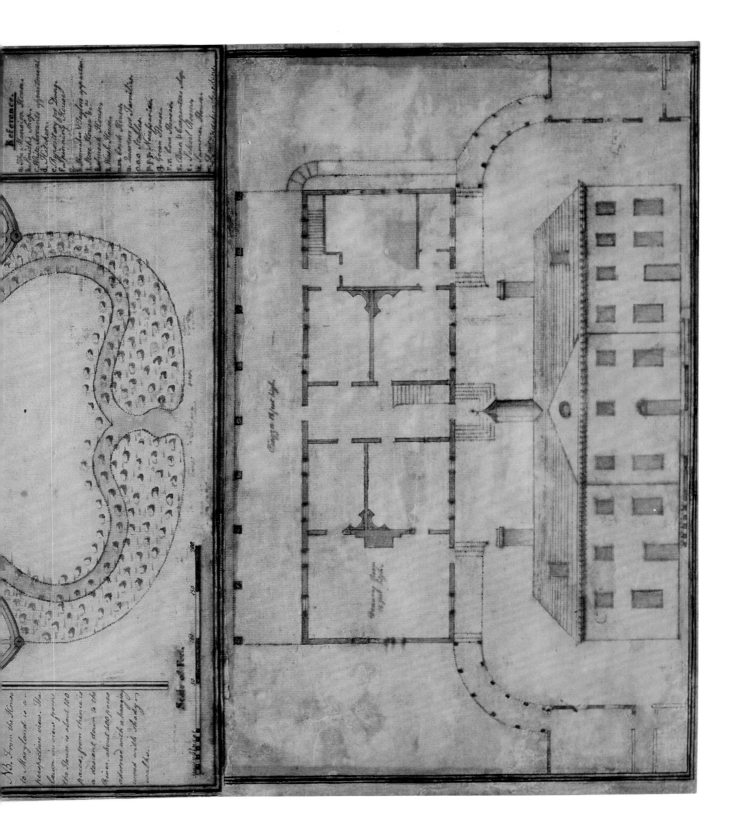

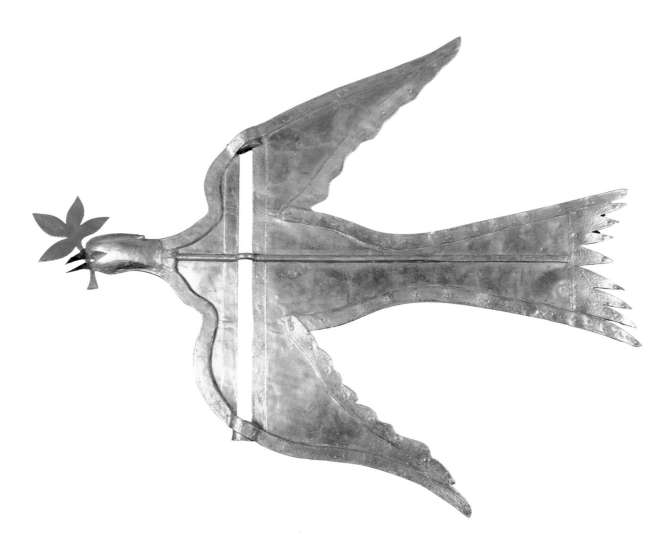

*Mount Vernon's unique dove of peace weathervane, with an olive branch in its beak, was made by Joseph Rakestraw. Washington ordered it in 1787, while he was presiding at the Constitutional Convention.*

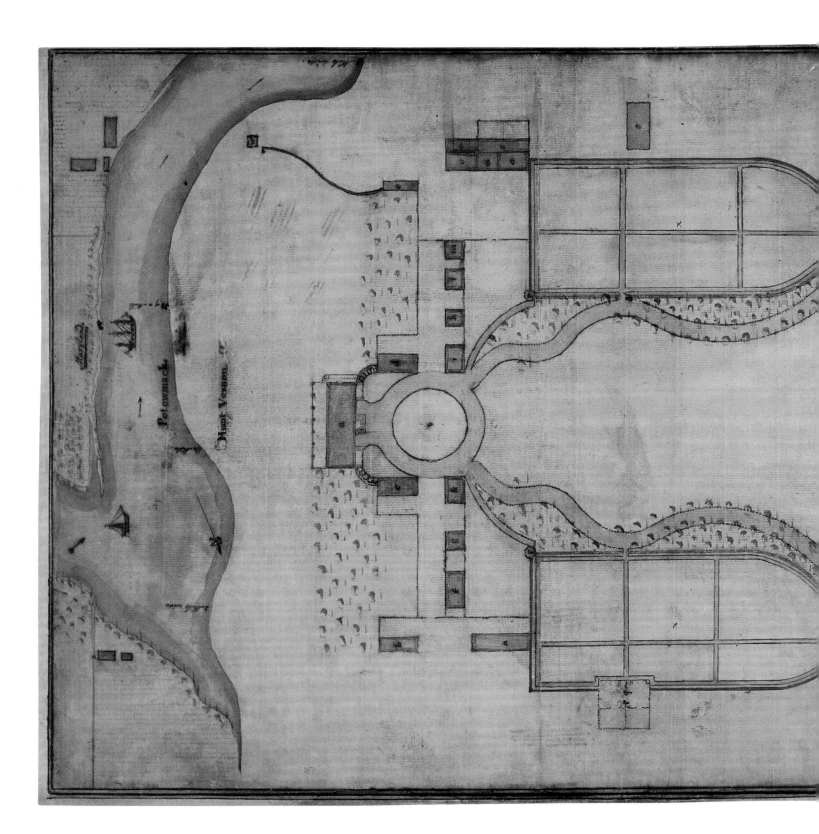

Maryland

Potowmack

Mount Vernon

Mt. Vernon-Garden.

# GEORGE WASHINGTON'S GARDENS

*Under the Watchful Eye of the Mount Vernon Ladies*

J. DEAN NORTON

*"Let one spot in this grand country of ours be saved from 'change!' Upon you rests this duty."*

Ann Pamela Cunningham, 1874

With the words quoted above, Mount Vernon Ladies' Association Regent Ann Pamela Cunningham presented a farewell challenge to the organization she had founded two decades earlier. Although this challenge might not sound especially difficult, the work of restoring and maintaining various structures as well as several hundred acres of historic gardens and landscapes has in fact proven quite complex. Over the past century and a half, the Ladies have dealt with many challenges, including the search for financial resources, lack of adequate historical information, and conflicts involving personal taste versus historical accuracy. Ultimately, their tireless efforts have elevated the "green side" of the estate to a level of beauty and historical accuracy that would have delighted Miss Cunningham.

Once the Ladies formally took possession of Mount Vernon, in February 1860, their immediate concern was to return the aging Mansion to its former glory. Their next priority was to deal with the outbuildings. A cleanup of the gardens would also be necessary, but that could be focused on properly at a later time. Even though a garden can decay quickly, with a little money and labor, it can be recovered and renewed much more easily than can deteriorating historic structures.

After George Washington's death, each successive family owner dealt with dwindling sources of funds and labor. Not surprisingly, the gardens deteriorated rapidly and quite visibly. As early as

*Postcard view of upper garden, circa 1900.*

1812 one visitor wrote, "[T]he garden is handsome, but I am told that it is nothing like what it was in the lifetime of the General."[1] Six years later, another visitor commented that the "whole place wears the appearance of decay and neglect in its present owner."[2] And in 1860, a newspaper correspondent reported: "The whole edifice is in a ruinous condition, and will have to be renovated from cupola to foundation. . . . The 'restoration' of the grounds has also been commenced, and it is to be hoped that soon the fine old garden will be put in order, and its ruined conservatory rebuilt."[3]

## Flowers

The gardens provided the Ladies' Association with a much-needed source of revenue in its early days. Even during the decades when George Washington's heirs still owned Mount Vernon, they had derived supplemental income from the sale of lemons and flowers from the gardens. Visitors recorded being able to "pluck" a lemon from one of Washington's trees or pull a "little bouquet from the blooming shrubbery."[4] In the 1860s, Sarah C. Tracy, Ann Pamela Cunningham's secretary, and Upton Herbert, Mount Vernon's first resident superintendent, shared responsibility for maintaining the estate. With limited funds available, Tracy took up the study of horticulture and cultivated roses and other flowers in great variety. On days when boats brought visitors, she was kept busy "tying up small bunches of flowers, which heaped in masses, were soon disposed of by the gardener at 25 cents, as souvenirs of Mount Vernon. These boat day profits served to defray the expense of keeping Mt. Vernon in good condition during the war."[5]

In 1881 the Ladies hired an experienced gardener, Franklin A. Whelan. He helped develop new sources of revenue from the gardens through the sale of seeds, cut flowers, plants, and fruits. The following year saw the printing of the first catalog of various plants for sale from Mount Vernon's gardens and greenhouses; roses were prominently listed. The minutes of the Association's annual meeting in 1883 underscored the financial significance of Mount Vernon's green spaces: "It is the sense of your committee that the Garden and Green-house can be, and bids fair to be, a lucrative source of income to the Association, and towards that end, they recommend that Council place the responsibility and accountability in the hands of the Gardener."[6]

A few years later, an opportunity emerged for the Ladies to participate in Washington, D.C.'s thriving cut-rose market. In 1888 a rose house was built at the east end of the upper garden—inspected and approved by rose growers from the District—and growing and selling commenced. In 1911 the committee on gardens and greenhouses reported that although the Ladies could not compete "with florists who raise roses and other flowers by the acre . . . we have succeeded in making the gardens one of the most attractive features at Mount Vernon."[7]

The sale of plants at Mount Vernon, which began in the early nineteenth century, continues today. They are no longer a major source of revenue but are considered a vivid element of a visit to the home of George Washington.

*Upper garden rose beds and greenhouse, 1970s.*

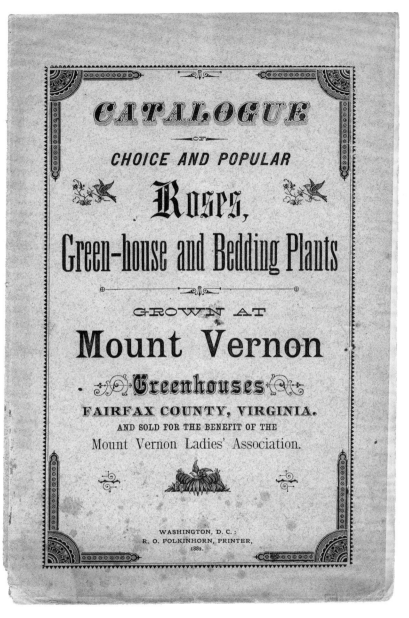

CATALOGUE
OF
CHOICE AND POPULAR
Roses,
Green-house and Bedding Plants
GROWN AT
Mount Vernon
Greenhouses
FAIRFAX COUNTY, VIRGINIA.
AND SOLD FOR THE BENEFIT OF THE
Mount Vernon Ladies' Association.

WASHINGTON, D. C.:
R. O. POLKINHORN, PRINTER,
1882.

ABOVE: *Mount Vernon's first garden and greenhouse sales catalog, 1882.* RIGHT: *John Ross Key painted this view of the upper garden around 1905.*

## Trees

George Washington loved trees. In his 1748 "Journal of my Journey over the Mountains," for example, he noted that "we went through the most beautiful Groves of Sugar Trees & spent the best part of the Day in admiring the Trees & richness of the Land."[8] Looking to redesign his country seat in 1785, he began searching for the "sort of Trees I shall want for my walks, groves, and Wilderness."[9] By the end of his life, he had planted hundreds of trees in these areas as well as on either side of the serpentine path near the Mansion.

Noting the condition of the landscape in the early 1870s, the Association reported: "Every effort has been made to put the place into a presentable condition, so that those who make the pilgrimage to the spot are no longer shocked by the ghastly traces of neglect and dilapidation."[10] One sure way to improve the appearance of the grounds was to undertake a program of tree planting and care as well as removal of distressed and dying trees. In 1899, in keeping with George Washington's fondness for introducing new varieties of ornamental trees to his pleasure grounds, several purple beech trees were planted. Although they were a handsome addition, they were historically inappropriate, as this type of beech had not been introduced to cultivation until after Washington's death.

In 1901 the Ladies sought the help of Charles Sprague Sargent, the esteemed director of Harvard's Arnold Arboretum, to examine the estate's trees for health, to suggest new plantings, and to identify trees that should be removed. Sargent initially refused, but he did send the Ladies a treatise on pruning forest and ornamental trees. The main difficulty for the Ladies proved to be finding "men willing to risk their lives climbing the largest trees."[11] Finally, in 1915, Sargent agreed to work with the Ladies, to their great delight. He accepted no payment, commenting that the "pleasure" of the task was "the only compensation I want."[12]

Between 1915 and his death in 1927, Sargent directed the clearing of the forest, the planting of thousands of new trees there and on the grounds, the removal of diseased or weak trees, and the care of many original and historic trees on the estate. He issued two reports, the first in 1917 and the second in 1926. In the introduction to his initial report, "The Trees at Mount Vernon," Sargent declared that "no trees planted by man have the human interest of the Mount Vernon trees. They belong to the nation and are one of its precious possessions. No care should be spared to preserve them."[13] This document mapped the locations of significant trees in the historic area, provided historical references for each species, and identified trees Sargent thought were survivals from Washington's time. He updated his first report in 1926, and the estate's staff continued to rely on this version for many years.[14]

A tremendous amount of arboricultural work occurred in the early twentieth century, including pruning, cabling, locating cavities in trees and scraping them clean, and drilling reinforcing rods through the trees and then filling the voids with concrete. Although these were the approved

*Mansion seen from a 145-foot-tall tulip poplar tree (one of two that George Washington planted on either side of the bowling green), 2009.*

practices of the time, many of them did more harm than good. One beneficial exception was the installation of lightning rods on all the larger trees—under the direction of Thomas A. Edison. Today, professional arborists employ the latest equipment, technology, and laboratory research to care for the trees at Mount Vernon; all the larger ones are climbed and inspected annually.

For decades, the estate staff used Sargent's 1926 report to determine which trees were original, that is, the ones that had been growing since Washington's lifetime. Then in 2005, a team of dendro-chronologists visited Mount Vernon, and besides coring beams of buildings to determine their age, they checked the thirteen trees thought to be original, based on Sargent's report. Unfortunately, this study ascertained that only five of these were in fact original: two huge tulip poplars standing on either side of the bowling green outside each garden gate; a Canadian hemlock just west of the upper garden gate; a white mulberry just outside the upper garden wall, adjacent to the gardener's seed-and-tool house; and a swamp chestnut oak on the Mansion's east slope. (This ancient tree fell in the spring of 2014.) When the scientists cored more specimen trees on the property and counted their rings, they found ten additional trees from the eighteenth century or earlier; the old-est, a chestnut oak, dated to before 1683. These trees are located within the forest surrounding the historic area at Mount Vernon and are not within public view.

LEFT: *Annual inspection of one of the two original tulip poplars, 2009.* OPPOSITE LEFT: *Charles Sprague Sargent's 1926 diagram of trees near the Mansion.* OPPOSITE RIGHT: *The work of an early 20th-century arborist at Mount Vernon.*

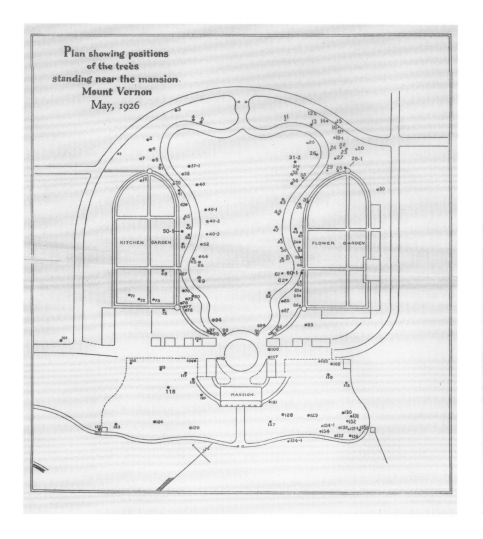

Plan showing positions
of the trees
standing near the mansion.
Mount Vernon
May, 1926

KITCHEN GARDEN

FLOWER GARDEN

MANSION

Coffee Bean #89

356

## Landscape Architecture

Concerning the broader landscape at Mount Vernon, beyond the garden walls, the Ladies' intention was always to replant, restore, and accurately represent the bowling green, shrubberies, wilderness areas, and groves. Assisting them in this undertaking were two Harvard-educated landscape architects, who arrived on the scene in 1932. Professor Morley Jeffers Williams and Harold T. Abbott established a systematic course of action to ensure that "whatever is done to modify the appearance of the grounds should be done in accordance with a preconceived plan." Their holistic approach to the landscape was ahead of its time. The "Mount Vernon estate," they wrote, "should be treated as a unit and all landscape features should be in terms of this plan."[15]

Over the years since then, historically inappropriate features and plants have been removed from the landscape, and plants cultivated in the eighteenth century have been added. In 1998 the Ladies accepted an offer by the Garden Club of Virginia to support the creation of an enhanced and accurate plan for the bowling green. Rudy Favretti, the club's landscape architect, worked with the Ladies to draw up and implement a program for improving the plantings within the shrubberies that surround the green. The Ladies hope to collaborate with the Garden Club again in the near future, with the goals of reviewing work on the bowling green, performing archaeological excavations for the "labyrinth of paths" in Washington's wilderness areas, and trying to locate six "ovals" that he created in 1792 using plants from the nursery John Bartram had founded south of Philadelphia. The aim is eventually to recreate the wildernesses and the elusive ovals, both important features of the estate's historic landscape.

*George Isham Parkyns's 1799 aquatint depicts the Mansion from the west— showing a ha-ha wall and tree plantings bordering the bowling green.*

# Lower Garden

George Washington's gardening realm was completed by the creation of kitchen, pleasure, and botanic gardens as well as a fruit garden and nursery. Throughout the Ladies' stewardship, all of Mount Vernon's gardens have been planted according to the prevailing historical understandings at a given time, drawing on details found in Washington's writings as well as on general perceptions about period gardens. In the Ladies' early years, of course, there was far less documentation to go on, and so it was much harder to ascertain what was truly appropriate. With the passage of time, other reliable sources of information have emerged to guide decisions about garden restoration.

For example, early twentieth-century images of the kitchen garden, located just south of the bowling green, show two terraces of long earthen beds planted with rows of vegetables. Scholarly research on this garden (called the lower garden in Washington's time and again today) began in 1934, when landscape architect Morley Jeffers Williams and Mount Vernon's assistant resident superintendent Charles Cecil Wall sought to create an authentic and permanent plan for that plot. In 1936 the Ladies' kitchen garden committee reported that the resulting plan for the space "was based on research and study of XVIII Century kitchen gardens."[16] Execution of the Williams and Wall plan was completed in 1937. Artist Nathalia Ulman's drawing of the space shows a beautiful terraced garden with herb-bordered vegetable beds, espaliered fruit trees, grapevines, berries, cisterns, and beehives. Copies of the plan were sent to "some very discriminating people, among whom were writers, artists and architects." These individuals responded with "genuine appreciation," and prints of Ulman's drawing were offered for sale to Mount Vernon visitors.[17]

The 1937 kitchen garden design was a product of the colonial revival landscape movement, which was then creating quite a stir in Colonial Williamsburg. The gardens there were recreated with geometric beds surrounded by brick walks and ubiquitous arbors. Herb borders, espaliers, and topiaries filled every garden area. As the Ladies' kitchen garden committee had noted in its 1936 report on the Williams-Wall plan, "Throughout the entire country there is a keen interest in period planting and herb growing."[18]

Debate continues today as to what should be done with Mount Vernon's lower garden. As an outstanding example of a formal English kitchen garden, it is a true colonial revival creation, one that strives for beauty as much as for historical accuracy. Given Washington's reputation for efficiency, one might expect that his kitchen garden would have had a simpler layout, with fewer paths and more ground devoted to the cultivation of large quantities of produce to feed his family and many guests. Should archaeologists dig up the garden looking for clues and then possibly return it to a much simpler layout? Or should the garden remain as it is, because it represents an important chapter in American landscape history and exemplifies the Ladies' historic-restoration efforts? These questions will be discussed at Mount Vernon for some time.

RIGHT: *Lower garden, 2007.*
OVERLEAF: *Lower garden, 1921.*

ABOVE: *Globe artichokes growing in lower garden.* RIGHT: The Kitchen Garden of Mount Vernon, *drawn by Nathalia Ulman in 1937.*

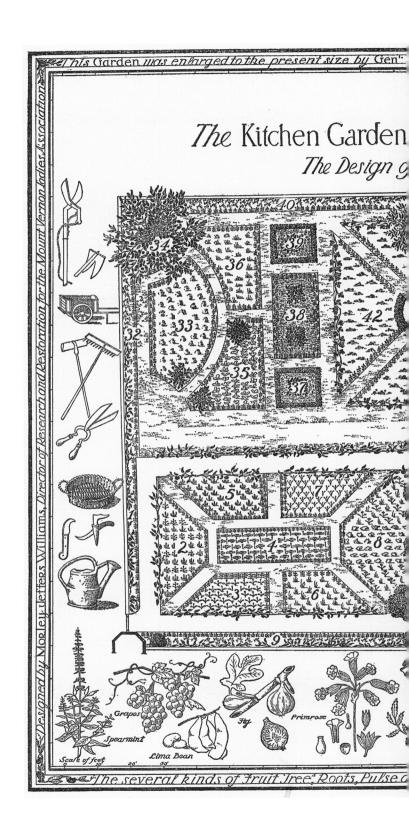

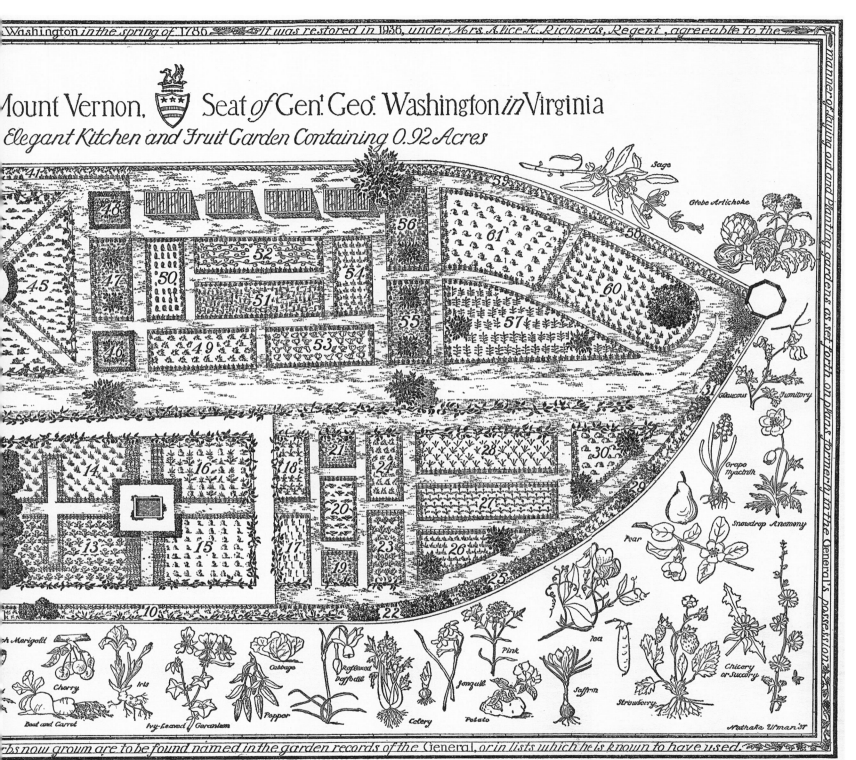

# Mount Vernon, Seat *of* Gen. Geo. Washington *in* Virginia

## Elegant Kitchen and Fruit Garden Containing 0.92 Acres

Sage

Globe Artichoke

Grape Hyacinth

Snowdrop Anemony

Pear

Glaucous Fumitory

Chicory or Succory

Strawberry

Tea

Pink

Jonquil

Saffron

Potato

Celery

Reflexed Daffodil

Pepper

Cabbage

Ivy-Leaved Geranium

Iris

Cherry

Beet and Carrot

Merigold

Nathalie Ulman '31

## A Horticulturalist Arrives

In 1946 the Ladies' Association created a new staff position, placing an advertisement for a horticulturist in *Horticulture* magazine. Robert B. Fisher filled the post and went on to spend more than forty years refining the eighteenth-century appearance of Mount Vernon's gardens and grounds. His dedication to accuracy was vividly demonstrated in 1974, when he ordered the removal of five hundred tulips that he recognized, as they bloomed, were not a type grown in Washington's time.

Around 1950, Fisher and Charles Cecil Wall, who was now the estate's resident director, co-authored "A List of Ornamental Trees and Shrubs Noted in the Writings of George Washington," a report that indicated where he had placed those plantings within his landscape.[19] In 1960 Fisher revised and expanded *The Mount Vernon Gardens*, a booklet originally compiled around 1941 by Mrs. Hetty Cary Harrison, Vice Regent for Virginia. Fisher's version included new information on the history and restoration of the gardens and grounds, together with tree, shrub, flower, fruit, and vegetable plant lists; the revised pamphlet was reprinted in 1973.[20]

## Botanical Garden

In 1982 Susanne Schrage, a student at Virginia Tech who was working as a summer intern at Mount Vernon to earn credit toward her horticulture degree, was asked to research the botanical garden to see if this small plot, just east of the upper garden, could be planted in a more historically accurate way. George Washington, who fondly called this space his "little garden," had sowed there a variety of new seeds, nuts and acorns of trees, shrubs, grasses, agricultural crops, and vegetables. Because of his great interest in this space, he kept detailed records of what was planted and where. Schrage's few months of research led to the creation of a new, more accurate plant list. Beds were rearranged, and where and when possible, plants were returned to the same beds they had occupied two centuries earlier.

*Botanical garden, 2007.*

## Upper Garden

As an increasing number of eighteenth-century documents became available for research and as interest grew in representing *all* the garden enclosures as accurately as possible, the Ladies' Association next focused attention on the upper garden. In 1984 Mount Vernon horticulturalist J. Dean Norton and Susanne Schrage (who was now the estate's boxwood gardener) began a major research project involving the upper garden. For a year, they consulted Washington's letters, diaries, and ledgers along with visitors' accounts, books in his library relating to horticulture or landscape, and period horticulture books that may have influenced his design decisions. Archaeologists dug a limited number of shovel test pits (one-by-one-foot square) and conducted a ground-penetrating radar study to survey the upper garden for physical evidence of eighteenth-century paths and beds. Unfortunately, this methodology was not sufficiently extensive to reveal the wealth of archaeological remains on the site. Norton and Schrage's report on their study, "The Upper Garden at Mount Vernon Estate, Its Past, Present, and Future: A Reflection of 18th-Century Gardening," was completed in the fall of 1985.

If there were ever a garden that exhibited restoration gone awry, it would be Mount Vernon's upper garden. Realizing that this plot had included flowers during George Washington's time, the Ladies took great personal interest in its appearance and, naturally, wanted it to be beautiful. In 1893 estate gardener Franklin A. Whelan reported that his idea was to "fill the garden with the old time plants and flowers so admired in years gone by."[21] Twelve years later, he wrote that "the multiplicity of plants and flowers will accentuate the beauty of our garden, already pronounced by competent authority (both foreign and native) to excel anything of its character in America today."[22]

In 1934 the Ladies' flower garden committee report noted, "Please bear in mind the fact that this garden is one of Mount Vernon's greatest assets."[23] The following year, Harold Abbott, who was now the estate's landscape architect, reported that

*Postcard view from 1926 showing upper garden and the greenhouse built in 1869.*

changes had been made "in an effort to approximate a flower garden typical of Washington's time. It should be kept in mind that the effect is not necessarily a restoration, there being practically no reference to the flowering herbaceous plants in the General's garden."[24] This assessment was valid: one problem facing researchers of the upper garden's history is that George Washington wrote very little about it. With its impressive greenhouse and flowers grown for beauty, not for use, this garden was surely intended to be the highlight of an eighteenth-century visitor's stroll about the pleasure grounds of the estate. However, Washington delegated to his gardener the planting and care of the upper garden; all he required of that individual was a weekly report, which focused on vegetables and the time spent performing various tasks.

The most significant alteration proposed in Norton and Schrage's 1985 report was the removal of two formal rose gardens created in the late nineteenth century.[25] Although the roses themselves were historically appropriate, the design of this pair of gardens was Victorian in nature and not in keeping with eighteenth-century design practices, which would have positioned roses throughout the garden within cultivated beds rather than concentrated and set apart. Norton and Schrage advocated replacing the two gardens with square and rectangular beds. The former west rose garden was planted with flowers, and the east side was planted with vegetables, a decision based on strong evidence that vegetables had predominated in that space during Washington's time.

Neither the ground-penetrating radar study nor the archaelogical test pits provided conclusive information about the state of other parts of the upper garden prior to 1799. Consequently, these were left untouched—in particular, four long borders and five crescent beds. The 1985 report ended with the thought that additional research would be necessary if a more historically accurate upper garden were to be created.

## Fruit Garden and Nursery

Washington's "Vineyard Inclosure" was the next area to be examined. During most of the twentieth century, it had been a mowed pasture with the occasional planting of cowpeas and other agricultural crops, plus six nursery beds containing boxwood and espaliered fruit trees. In the 1770s Washington had used this space, about four acres in size, to cultivate wine grapes; they soon failed. He then converted the area into a fruit garden and nursery. Ornamental plants that required more space than those in the botanical garden were grown here for use within the landscape; trees were grown to be used for creating living fences; grasses for the collection of seed; and vegetables for harvest.

The 1997 restoration of the fruit garden and nursery, which drew together archival and archaeological findings, exemplified a new level of interdisciplinary research. Washington's keen interest in this space had led him to keep detailed records of plant locations; for the first time, the written word

*Nursery beds, 2012.*  meshed beautifully with archaeological evidence unearthed during excavations that had begun in

1988. The remains of post holes from the post-and-rail fence, ditch lines dug for drainage, and fruit-tree root stains were consistent with the plan Washington described in his letters and diaries. With an accurate program in hand, horticulturalists were able to restore the fruit garden and nursery to its eighteenth-century design.

## Boxwood

The plant most often mentioned in Mount Vernon Ladies' Association records is the English box-wood, the preferred edging plant of the eighteenth century and one that Washington's gardeners had installed in the upper garden in November 1798. Boxwood was favored for its dwarf habit of growth and its tolerance of frequent shearing. (The dimensions recommended by eighteenth-century horticulturists for box edging were a mere three inches high by three inches wide.) Although dwarf English boxwood grows very slowly, usually less than an inch per year, it does continue to grow, and after a hundred years, it can easily reach heights of six to eight feet. For mid-twentieth-century admirers, mature boxwood evoked nostalgia, prompting one admirer to describe it as "a heritage from yesterday, a privilege for today and a bequest for tomorrow."[26]

The Ladies loved their English boxwood and did everything they could to preserve and protect it. But the plant caused constant worry. After the severe winter of 1899–1900, Regent Mrs. Howard Townsend wrote in her annual report, "The box fence I shall never see in its glory again, . . .

LEFT: *Overgrown boxwood along upper garden's center path, 1987.*
RIGHT: *The garden layout installed in the upper garden in 1985 contained 31 small beds and 24 paths. This geometric design was inspired by Batty Langley's* New Principles of Gardening *(1728).*

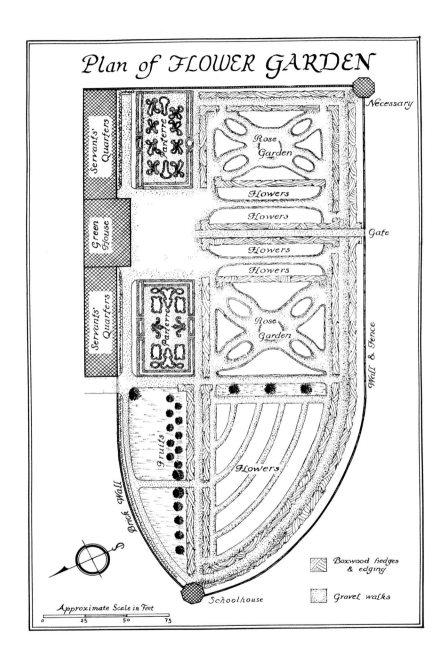

# Plan of FLOWER GARDEN

Servants' Quarters

Parterre

Green House

Servants' Quarters

Parterre

Brick Wall

Fruits

Rose Garden

Flowers

Flowers

Flowers

Flowers

Rose Garden

Flowers

Necessary

Gate

Wall & Fence

Schoolhouse

Boxwood hedges & edging

Gravel walks

Approximate Scale in Feet

0    25    50    75

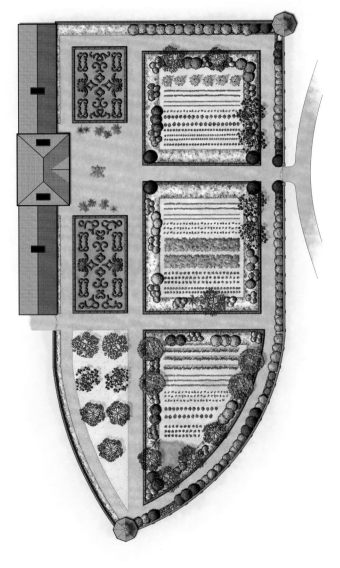

do all that is possible to reanimate it."[27] Seven years later the garden and greenhouse committee was both surprised and thrilled to declare that the "box hedges and shrubs were never more verdant and beautiful."[28]

For many years, Mount Vernon's boxwood was pruned formally—that is, in an angular boxlike shape. During World War II, however, manpower was in short supply on the estate, and formal shearing of the boxwood ceased. By 1978 the plantings were six feet tall and equally wide, and they were in dire need of attention. A boxwood-maintenance program was established with the hope of returning the hedges to their past glory. Unfortunately, an incurable disease—boxwood decline (*Paecilomyces buxi*)—began attacking the plant along the East Coast during the 1970s. As a result, by 2005 few of Mount Vernon's once lush English box hedges remained.

## The Upper Garden Revisited

Sad as it was to see the boxwood decline, it did afford a perfect opportunity for archaeologists to re-enter the upper garden in 2005 and conduct an excavation more extensive than the isolated shovel test pits that had been dug during the 1985 study of the enclosure. Amazingly, the ensuing five-year excavation uncovered evidence for the entire two hundred-fifty-year span of the garden. Most significantly, the archaeologists found no evidence that walks had existed within the large main beds of the 1799 garden. This eliminated the possibility that there had been the multiple small square and crescent-shaped beds that generations of gardeners had imposed on the space.

The research and restoration of any outdoor space can be likened to solving a word puzzle. Despite the availability of primary documentation, gardeners prior to 2005 were, in effect, trying to solve the upper garden puzzle without having the vowels. The archaeologists' findings provided the vowels. Their discoveries enabled Mount Vernon scholars to revisit and interpret past research with a new set of eyes.

In 1796, when the architect Benjamin Henry Latrobe described what he had seen at Mount Vernon as "a neat flower garden laid out in squares, and boxed with great precission," he was referring to large squares—not numerous small squared beds.[29] Following classic design principles for pleasure gardens consisting of only a few acres, eighteenth-century horticulturists and designers suggested combining the necessary parts of gardening with pleasure. What the excavations of 2005 through 2010 revealed was that Washington, like many of his contemporaries, had followed this design concept. Large areas cultivated for vegetables were bordered with flowers, roses, fruit trees, and shrubs. The pleasure garden, then, was actually the border surrounding the vegetable beds.

In August 2010 the upper garden beds south of the central straight path were scraped away, the ten-foot-wide eighteenth-century paths were restored, and the upper garden of George and Martha Washington reemerged. Without a doubt, this was the most exciting garden restoration in Mount

LEFT: *Upper garden plan by Worth Bailey, 1940.* RIGHT: *Upper garden restoration plan, 2010.*

TOP: *Boxwood decline takes its toll, 2009.*
BOTTOM: *Removal of small crescent beds,*
*2010.* RIGHT: *Last traces of the small*
*flower beds, 2010.*

Vernon's history. New archaeological methodology and physical evidence had informed the interpretation of the voluminous primary documentation. Findings were shared with archaeological and horticultural experts, and the outcome was deemed a one-of-a-kind historically accurate garden restoration.

Achieving historical accuracy in Mount Vernon's landscape and garden spaces has always been a goal of the Ladies' Association—but not always the result. Today, there is still much to be done. While debate continues over the interpretation of the kitchen garden, plans are in place for other important work, including extensive tree plantings to fill in the groves, especially the south grove; restoration of the wilderness area; and locating, and then restoring, the mysterious six oval beds. More than two hundred years after George Washington's death, research continues. The final chapter will never be written, but excitement is high as efforts continue to preserve, protect, and maintain his home for future generations.

*New large square beds in upper garden, 2014.*

# "LAID OUT IN SQUARES, AND BOXED WITH GREAT PRECISSION"

*Uncovering George Washington's Upper Garden*

ESTHER C. WHITE

*Excavation of western end of upper garden, 2009. A series of trenches running diagonally across the site provide evidence of the extensive soil preparation done to bring this part of the garden into cultivation during the late 1780s and 1790s.*

Since the death of George Washington in 1799, visitors have traveled to Mount Vernon to see his home, explore the grounds, and pay their respects to his memory. The landscape—and especially the walled gardens flanking the bowling green on the west side of the Mansion—is an especially meaningful component of the visitor experience. Numerous accounts testify to visitors' convictions that the upper garden—the northern of the two gardens—had held special meaning for General Washington and that it was a place where his character remained especially apparent. With its imposing brick greenhouse, it is felt to be a testament to Washington's expertise in nurturing natural beauty and bringing life from the rich soil of the nation.

In 2011 the Mount Vernon Ladies' Association unveiled a restoration of Washington's upper garden. This reinterpreted and newly configured space showcased the results of a multiyear, interdisciplinary program designed to uncover, both literally and figuratively, the layout and appearance of the garden in 1799. Mount Vernon's horticulturalists and archaeologists spent five years meticulously researching, excavating, and analyzing findings, uncovering new evidence and gaining new insights into one of the most cherished spaces at Washington's estate.[1]

This research effort began when the six-foot-tall boxwood hedges flanking the garden paths sickened. Their demise was due to a combination of factors—primarily poor drainage, disease, and insect infestations—that together have been given the prosaic name of "boxwood decline." After numerous efforts to stem the rate of decline proved unsuccessful, it became clear that the plantings' days were numbered, and that their passing would provide an opportunity for research and the ability to make changes to the overall design of the upper garden.[2] Samples of the existing boxwood's trunks were polished and photographed under a microscope by historic-paint analyst Susan Buck, providing an enlarged image of the growth rings. Counting the magnified rings proved that the boxwood had been planted about 1850.[3] The discovery that the plants did not date to George Washington's day considerably eased the difficult decision to remove all the boxwood and start over.

The results of the interdisciplinary research endeavor to uncover the history of the upper garden proved to be much more complex and fascinating than anyone had imagined. At the outset, the major concern was whether any evidence for earlier layouts of the garden survived for the archaeologists to study. As the space had been continuously cultivated since Washington's passing, it was feared that the soil layers and the gravel paths marking earlier garden beds and walkways might have been completely obliterated through the continuous cultivation of the area. However, there proved to be not only extensive physical evidence for Washington's 1799 layout in the upper garden but also physical and documentary evidence for at least five additional garden designs, stacked one on top of another, waiting to be uncovered. The meticulous excavation of these strata revealed the evolution of the upper garden and disclosed details about how the interpretation of this one-acre plot through the previous two centuries had embodied changing interpretations of George Washington himself.

*Upper garden and greenhouse, 2013. The greenhouse is once again the focal point when one enters the garden from the bowling green gate.*

## Two Colonial-Period Phases

On March 21, 1763, George Washington recorded in his diary, "Grafted 40 Cherrys . . . 12 Magnum Bonum Plums" in rows starting "next the Quarter." This reference, interpreted as indicating the "house for families" slave quarter located adjacent to the upper garden, suggests that cultivation in the upper garden had begun by this date.[4] This garden on the north side of the Mansion mirrored that of the slightly earlier garden to the south: these two symmetrical plots were rectangular enclosures of about an acre, oriented from north to south, surrounded by brick walls and separated by a central drive. Small, frame octagonal structures were built at the center points of the eastern and western walls of both gardens—"necessaries" (outhouses) along the eastern walls and houses for storing tools and seeds along the western walls. The upper garden, or "new garden," as Washington called it, seems to have been primarily a fruit and nut nursery, with some cultivation of vegetables and even flower knots mentioned in his references to activities in this space.

The archaeological evidence supports this interpretation of the earliest two phases of gardening. Numerous examples of two distinct types of archaeological features were uncovered for these phases. The earliest ones dated to the 1760s and consisted of rectangular holes ranging from approximately three by four feet to four by five feet and were thought to be plantings for young trees. The second consisted of long, linear beds, less than three feet wide, interpreted as beds for vegetables. The rectangular tree holes looked to have been laid out in orderly rows with no overlap upon one another. There were also no signs of root growth found in the bottoms of the excavated holes. These three characteristics suggest that the young trees were planted with an overall systematic scheme, rather than haphazardly, and that the specimens were not in these holes very long, at least not long enough for their root systems to grow into the undisturbed subsoil. Two gaps in the layout of these rectangular features suggest there might have been walkways between clusters or groupings of trees.

One of the linear features intrudes into a rectangular tree hole, suggesting that the vegetable beds were slightly later additions, perhaps from the 1770s, but the linear beds appear to have coexisted simultaneously with the tree holes during the 1770s and 1780s. Four groupings of linear beds were uncovered, one to the east and the others near the center of the garden. In all cases, these long beds appear to have served as a border of vegetables surrounding rows of young trees.

Based upon our current understanding of the layout of the early garden, there could be two hundred or more of these rectangular tree holes, with spaces between sections suggesting that walkways or paths existed between groupings of young trees. Washington's diary references to the garden in the 1760s and early 1770s are heavily devoted to the transplanting, grafting, and nurturing of trees in this space; sometimes the relocation of dozens of trees is noted in a single entry. For example, on March 10, 1775, he recorded transplanting grafts of several species of cherry trees "next the Quarter," including "13 May Duke & next to those 12 Black May Cherry . . . 6 Cornation, and 6 May Cherry," followed the next day with "5 Peach Kernals . . . 130 Peaches . . . 25 Missisippi Nuts."[5]

TOP LEFT: *The archaeologists found numerous rectangular features identified as evidence for the transplanting of fruit and nut trees in the earliest 1760s garden.* BOTTOM LEFT: *These long trenches are thought to have been beds for vegetables planted in the 1770s and 1780s.* RIGHT: *Archaeologists uncover the 1799 garden's perimeter path, 2010.*

# The 1799 Garden

Just before the outbreak of the Revolutionary War, George Washington embarked on a major campaign to enlarge the Mansion and reorganize the outbuildings and lanes surrounding his home. Besides this restructuring of the built environment, he also conceived an ambitious plan to adopt fashionable English landscape ideas to complement the new structures and, ultimately, to remodel his landscape. Although Washington began this transformation of his estate before taking command of the Continental Army in June 1775, his absence and shortages caused by the war prolonged the overall project. Most of the landscape alterations were not begun until he returned home in December 1783, after resigning his military commission. The completed landscape is therefore closely identified with the Washington who had taken his place upon the world stage.

The initial phase of the reorganization began in the mid-1770s with a major building campaign that eventually almost doubled the size of the Mansion and replaced four main outbuildings with a line of structures positioned along newly created lanes that met at the carriage circle on the west side of the house. Washington's correspondence with his plantation manager and cousin, Lund Washington, illuminates the scale of this project as well as both men's frustration over the difficulty of having to communicate via letters in order to implement the general's vision for Mount Vernon's core.

Two instances suggest that Washington's larger landscape plan was formed in his own mind, if not completely communicated to others, before his extended absence. On August 19, 1776, in the midst of the Long Island campaign, he wrote to Lund with detailed instructions on planting groves at either end of the Mansion. The letter is quite specific about the general's desire for locusts on the north and on the south, "clever" trees that would blossom, such as crab apples and dogwoods, and "these Trees to be Planted without any order or regularity"; it also specifies the route of the fence enclosing the east lawn.[6] These projects were not undertaken until the spring of 1785, when Washington was directly supervising the ongoing landscape work.[7]

The second indication that George Washington's larger landscape design was embedded as part of the overall system of alterations is a question posed by Lund on November 12, 1775, regarding the construction of a wall in the upper garden. "I think I have heard you say you design[e]d to have a House Built the whole length for Negroes," Lund wrote, and then suggested that "perhaps you may direct that to be first done" to make the garden wall construction more integrated.[8] A version of the "house" to which Lund referred became one of the final components of the reorganized plantation landscape—the slave quarter wings completed during the winter of 1792–93, to the east and west of the greenhouse.

Whether Washington's picturesque landscape is viewed as one complete system (as proposed here) or as a phased approach (as Adam Erby suggests in his chapter "Designing the Beautiful"), there is no question of the transformative impact this vision had upon the Mount Vernon grounds.

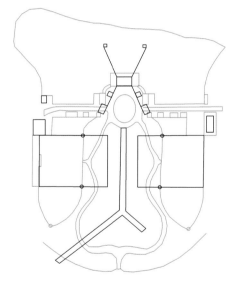

ABOVE: *The early layout of Mount Vernon (black) and the later redesigned landscape (green).* RIGHT: *Samuel Vaughan's 1787 presentation drawing of the Mansion and its surroundings (detail).* OVERLEAF: *Upper garden from the northwest, 2014.*

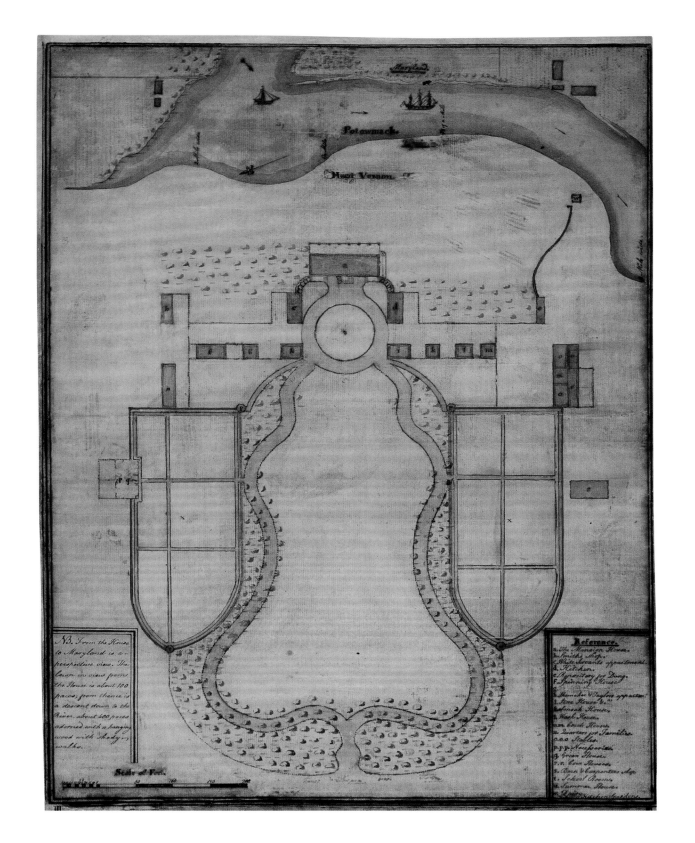

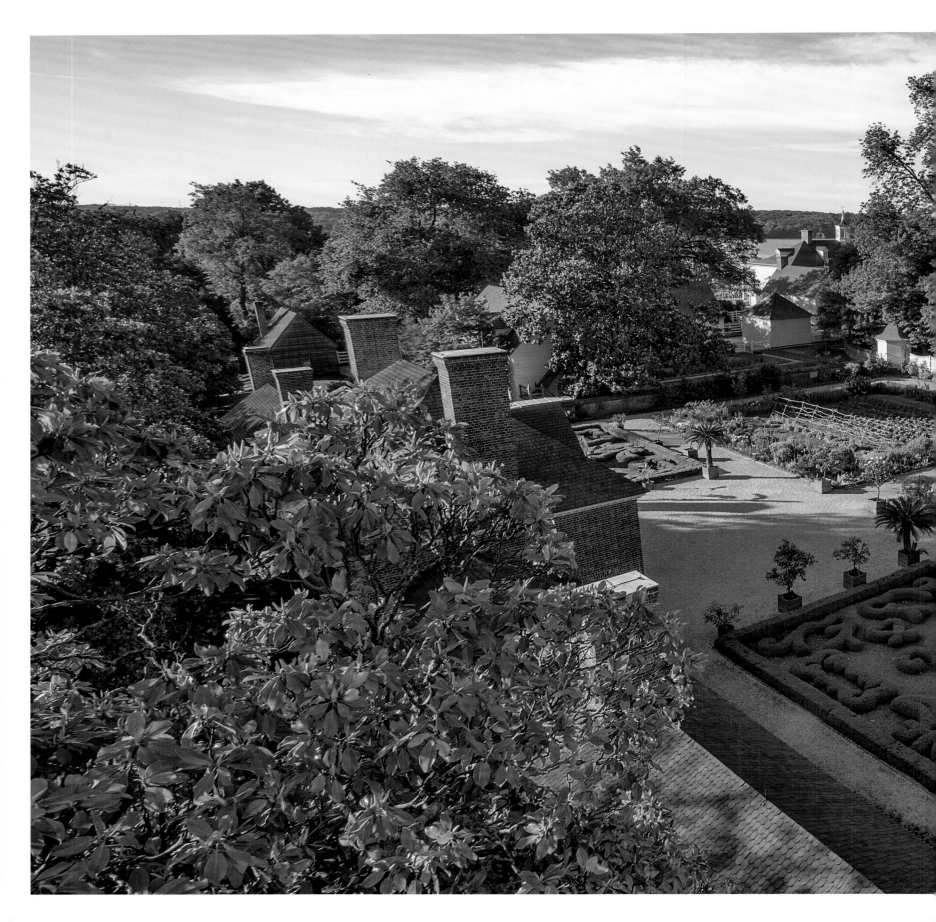

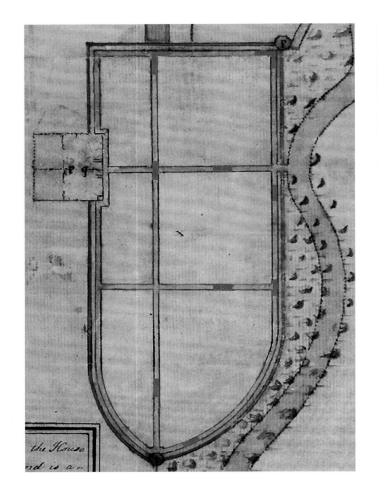

*Modern path*

*19th-century path*

*Brown loam with brick, the 1790s garden topsoil*

*Mottled silty clay "double digging"*

*Rectangular planting feature*

Landscape work west of the Mansion began after Washington's victorious return, when his presence at Mount Vernon after an eight-year absence found him personally directing the processes of moving earth—to construct the broad bowling green and meandering serpentine walk that would embellish the approach to the house—as well as riding his lands seeking trees and plants to move to the various areas being created. To make way for the bowling green, the walls of the flanking rectangular gardens were shifted and reconfigured so as to enclose longer, narrower spaces—shield-shaped gardens, realigned to an east-west axis. This is the version of the upper garden that was present in 1799. Documenting, restoring, and interpreting that garden for the one million tourists who visit Mount Vernon annually was the primary research goal of the 2005–10 interdisciplinary investigation.

Besides the rich archaeological evidence uncovered, several other sources were instrumental in understanding the layout of the upper garden during the final years of George Washington's life. In 1787, while Washington was presiding over the Constitutional Convention in Philadelphia, an English friend, Samuel Vaughan, visited Mount Vernon and recorded its reordered landscape in his journal. He later refined this sketch in a presentation drawing that he sent to the general.[9] Regarded as the best illustration of the overall landscape Washington implemented after the Revolutionary War, Vaughan's depiction provided an important primary document for the most recent re-analysis and restoration of the upper garden. His sketch and formal drawing label *both* the upper and lower gardens as "Kitchen Garden," suggesting that the dichotomy by which we understand the two gardens today (with the upper being a more formal space with flowers and the lower a kitchen garden cultivating fruits and vegetables) had not yet occurred in 1787.

It is also in the 1780s that accounts by visitors to Mount Vernon begin with regularity, becoming another important primary source for interpreting the plantation landscape.[10] Not surprisingly, there are often contradictions in these accounts. Guests to the estate inevitably viewed the home of George Washington through lenses that filtered in their notions of his achievements, his character, and his contributions to the nation. Visits just a few months apart could paint vastly different pictures, presumably in part reflecting broader perceptions about the man, and, after his death, incorporating expressions about the maintenance and upkeep of the revered leader's estate.

OPPOSITE LEFT: *The locations of the wide, graveled paths uncovered by archaeologists, marked in red on Samuel Vaughan's 1787 drawing of the upper garden.* OPPOSITE RIGHT: *A cross-section of the layers discovered in the later pathway areas of the upper garden.* RIGHT: *A thick layer of gravel marks the original ten-foot-wide path from the bowling green gate, beneath the narrower modern path.*

These contradictions are quite striking in visitor accounts from the 1790s, and provide clues to the metamorphosis that occurred in the upper garden over that decade. During this period, Washington's picturesque landscape was in its infancy. His upper garden was gradually evolving from the kitchen garden that Vaughan recorded in 1787 to a more formal space befitting the large, two-story brick greenhouse, constructed between 1784 and 1787, that was the focal point. In 1793 Winthrop Sargent wrote of "Kitchen and Flower Gardens," the first time the upper and lower gardens were so distinguished. Having served the government for several years in Ohio Territory, Sargent was impressed by Mount Vernon's grounds, remarking on the substantial greenhouse that sheltered "valuable exotics."[11] Three years later, the English-born architect Benjamin Henry Latrobe presented less-glowing reviews of the garden. Familiar with the great, landed estates of England, Latrobe saw only a "plain greenhouse" sheltering "nothing very rare," and he remarked on the archaic nature of the general's parterre.[12]

The recent archaeological excavations reconciled the contradictory nature of these accounts, revealing the extensive remodeling of the upper garden during the move to a naturalistic landscape as well as the continued reliance on geometric-shaped beds within the garden proper (rather than the curved, flowing lines or surprises one might expect to see in a garden set within a picturesque landscape). The archaeologists uncovered a layer of soil that suggests extensive earth moving was undertaken to prepare the garden for the changes that occurred during the late 1780s and early 1790s. This layer, found throughout the realigned garden, has a distinctive, silty, mottled appearance. It is interpreted as evidence of "double digging," the act of mixing and preparing the soil for cultivation. This evidence was one of the hallmarks facilitating identification of the 1799 upper garden. In the eastern end, which had been cultivated since the 1760s, this thick layer of soil served as a break between the earlier rectangular and linear features and later modifications. In contrast, this was the earliest layer seen in the western end of the garden, an area that was newly brought under cultivation with the creation of the shield-shaped layout. In the western end, the trenching associated with double digging was clearly defined. Individual trenches were approximately a foot wide and spaced less than half a foot apart.

The physical evidence suggests that during the 1790s the upper garden contained three large squared beds surrounded by wide gravel paths, laid out to provide striking views of the greenhouse from almost any vantage point but especially as one entered from the serpentine walk along the bowling green. This simple geometrical layout contrasted with the naturalistic principles guiding the larger landscape design outside the garden walls. The foundation of this geometric plan remained embedded within the three versions of the upper garden that evolved through the nineteenth and twentieth centuries, but these later gardens were increasingly subjected to naturalistic principles in an effort to showcase Washington's talents as the designer of the Mount Vernon landscape.

The gravel paths comprised another important archaeological finding from the 1799 garden. Remnants of these pathways were composed of a distinctive mixture of red clay and gravel and

*An excavation unit at the junction of the upper garden's main north-south and east-west paths confirmed their width and location, 2009.*

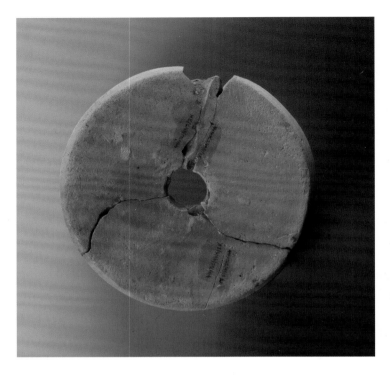

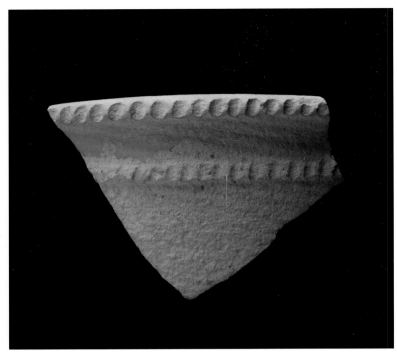

were well preserved in a number of places below as many as twenty layers of later path material. The archaeological evidence for the 1790s paths aligned remarkably well with their locations as shown on Samuel Vaughan's 1787 presentation drawing. Furthermore, when archaeologists excavated within the many existing pathways that were not shown on that drawing, the distinctive eighteenth-century layers were absent, clearly indicating that the non-Vaughan paths were later additions.

The archaeologists also determined that all the 1799 paths ranged in width from at least five feet to more than ten feet, much wider than the later iterations. The widest paths followed the intended circulation route, around the perimeter of the middle of the three large beds. Vaughan's drawing illustrates the three primary axial paths: one running from the bowling green gate to the principal facade of the greenhouse, between the eastern and center planting beds; a parallel path between the center and western beds; and a path running along the garden's east-west axis to the octagonal garden house located at the point where the curved walls meet. This third path served as the division between the northern boundary of the three planting beds and the orchard area and boxwood parterres located in the northern section of the upper garden. A secondary path went around the perimeter of the entire garden, and its narrower width suggested it was intended for use by gardeners rather than visitors.

The linear boundary for the three planting beds of the 1799 upper garden was visible for more than twenty feet in several places throughout the space, always next to a corresponding path. The archaeologists quickly discovered that the best areas to study the 1799 garden were below early nineteenth-century paths where these served to cap and seal the layers underneath.

The addition of multiple pathways, which began in the two decades following Washington's death and continued through the nineteenth and twentieth centuries, was probably a direct correlation to the growth of the boxwood hedges. Eighteenth-century gardening texts, such as Thomas Mawe and John Abercrombie's *Universal Gardener and Botanist* (1778), called for boxwood borders to be pruned to maintain a diminutive size, between six and eight inches high.[13] However, the boxwood borders planted after Washington's death were allowed to grow tall and wide, following later custom. These expansive plantings forced once-wide paths to become constricted and narrow. The solution was to create additional paths, often paralleling the original ones, in order to provide access throughout the beds. Both the old and new paths became much narrower, obscuring the open plan of the 1799 garden. The intended views within the space, particularly of the greenhouse, were eclipsed by massive boxwood, often identified by delighted visitors as a maze, a feature that was never intended to be part of the general's garden.

*Eighteenth-century flowerpot fragments recovered in upper garden excavations have a characteristic double-rolled rim with rouletted design and incised swags around the body.*

Patience was essential in pinpointing one historic garden within the continuum of a living garden, one that had been actively cultivated for more than two centuries. To identify a specific period among all the earlier and later gardens, especially the additions that occurred after Washington's death, as well as to understand the cultural implications embodied within the space through time, required a nuanced methodology grounded in deciphering multiple gardens within the space.

## The Garden of the Later Washington Families

With each decade that passed after George Washington's death, the details in visitors' accounts of Mount Vernon became more tenuous, reflecting the near-divine nature of his image. It is clear that visitors found it increasingly difficult to analyze and weigh how this pervasive image influenced their experiences in the upper garden. During the first half of the nineteenth century, they inevitably wrote about a trinity of hallowed sites—the Mansion, the tomb, and the upper garden.[14] As the century progressed, there was a marked evolution in these accounts, and the upper garden emerged during this time as a tangible reminder of Washington's image, a place with a direct connection to the man himself, a spot he had carefully crafted, a reflection of his aesthetic sense and Cincinnatus-like character.

During the early 1800s, the image of Washington in the garden was nurtured by the gardeners, enslaved workers brought to Mount Vernon by Washington's nephew and heir, Bushrod Washington, who owned the plantation from 1802 until his death in 1829. These gardeners were often the only people visitors encountered.[15] They told evocative stories about the plant species General Washington had personally nurtured, and visitors embraced his status as the modern classical hero returning from battle to take up the simple pursuit of gardening, exchanging his sword for a trowel, spade, and hoe. A journal entry written by Bostonian Caroline Moore after her 1833 visit is typical for this time, recording a garden she believed to be little changed from the one Washington had created: "[W]e saw a Sago tree, which was planted by the General's own hand as the Gardener said."[16]

Plantation documents from the first half of the nineteenth century, combined with the archaeological record, indicate that the upper garden was vastly different from the one George Washington had fashioned yet was also a space he might have recognized—even if he had not planted the lemons or sago palm himself.[17] Bushrod Washington constructed three additional buildings on the northern boundary of the upper garden: a pisé, or rammed-earth (similar to adobe) greenhouse three feet west of his uncle's greenhouse and slave quarter complex, and two brick buildings identified as a hothouse and a pinery (a greenhouse for the cultivation of pineapples).[18] These two brick structures were built one foot south of the slave quarter wings.[19] It is interesting to note that visitors during and immediately after Bushrod's tenure suggested that the garden was one place that did not seem to be in disrepair. These statements, combined with the structural evidence, imply that Bushrod invested heavily in the upper garden, enhancing a space that visitors projected as being George's creation rather than Bushrod's.

Archaeological excavation has yielded glimpses of the foundations of Bushrod's three buildings as well as strata that imply that even as he was clearly undertaking greatly expanded and specialized gardening activities, he probably did not radically alter the overall structure of his uncle's garden. The same large geometric beds and paths persisted through the early nineteenth century,

Washington the Farmer, *an illustration from Joel T. Headley's* Life of George Washington *(1856).*

RUINS OF THE CONSERVATORY AND SERVANTS' QUARTERS.

although during Bushrod's tenure the number of paths increased, slightly diminishing the size of the three main planting beds.

An 1833 inventory of the upper garden provides a detailed and intriguing glimpse into the plants being cultivated four years after Bushrod's death. At this time, the property was owned by Jane Blackburn Washington (tenure: 1832–41), the widow of Bushrod's nephew and heir, John Augustine Washington II (tenure: 1829–32). This inventory only describes plants in pots and boxes, but the numbers are striking: 460 pots of flowers, including 78 geraniums; and 108 boxes and tubs being cultivated with lemons, sweet and bitter oranges, magnolia, and shaddock, an Asian species similar to grapefruit. Nowhere in this handwritten account is there any mention of specimens as having been planted by George Washington's hands.[20]

Just two years after this inventory was taken, a fire destroyed George Washington's brick greenhouse and probably also severely damaged Bushrod Washington's immediately adjacent hothouse and pinery. This catastrophe initiated a distinct change in the tone and character of visitor accounts. From 1835 onward, the greenhouse ruins created a romantic backdrop for the reverent regard of the first president's garden. Yet the fire also had a symbolic impact, embodying the overall decline of the plantation that had begun in 1829 with the death of both Bushrod and his wife; later Washingtons lacked the immense resources necessary to maintain the estate.[21]

LEFT: *Ruins of George Washington's greenhouse and slave quarter, illustrated by Benson Lossing in 1859.* RIGHT: *Bushrod Washington's pisé greenhouse, circa 1862.*

## The Mount Vernon Ladies' Association

Washington family ownership ended in 1860, when the purchase of two hundred acres of the plantation by the Mount Vernon Ladies' Association was finalized. One of the Ladies' early tasks was cleaning up and restoring the upper garden's paths and brick walls, probably made necessary in large part by the continued popularity of the garden and the profits to be gained from selling flowers and plants.[22] This emphasis on cultivation for profit continued after the Civil War with the construction in 1869 of three garden structures, including a new greenhouse over the remains of George Washington's original building.[23] Garden sales catalogs, listing more than eighty species, began to be printed in 1882, providing valuable revenue for the young Association.

Visitors responded positively to the Ladies' gardening endeavors, imagining that the upper garden was, increasingly, reflective of the eighteenth century despite the presence, by 1896, of a grapery, carnation house, rose house, palm house, and "modern" propagating house to support commercial sales. The Association's early period also brought modifications to the infrastructure of the upper garden, usually with the aim of improving the visitor's experience, with plank walkways for strolling, benches, and interpretive signs. As period images show, the upper garden of the late nineteenth century was a Victorian-influenced space, with additional paths and exotic roses grown within the confines of Washington's two main squared beds, and five new crescent-shaped beds carved out of his third large planting bed, at the western end of the garden.

These entrepreneurial and infrastructural changes are visible in the archaeological record as well, providing benchmarks that aid in dating the stratigraphy and facilitating the task of pinpointing one specific garden within the multiple gardens that existed. Efforts to improve the soil through boring and drainage during this period left small round holes and distinctive loose, granular material in these late-nineteenth-century layers. The creation of the crescent beds destroyed earlier layers of the garden's history but preserved a complete cross-section of garden strata below the five curved paths bounding these beds.

The Ladies' efforts in the upper garden and their focus on both profit and beauty within its walls helped to retain the prominence of this spot through the organization's early decades. Visitors ventured into the garden seeking assurance that the space was a faithful version of the garden Washington had known, and thus could provide the intimate connection they prized with the memory of the first president. Imagined images of him in his garden became popular during the late nineteenth and early twentieth centuries. These images helped to authenticate the Ladies' activities as well as to propagate the idea of Washington as the nurturer of plants, domestic tranquility, and democracy—values that the Association sought strongly to align with him during this period.

Among the most popular of these images was *Washington in the Garden at Mount Vernon*, by the Brandywine River school artist Howard Pyle. He illustrated a series of biographical sketches

*The upper garden paths were covered with wooden planking from 1899 to 1902.*

ABOVE: *In this stereoscopic view taken before 1881, an unidentified Mount Vernon employee stands at the upper garden gate, with the greenhouse built by the Ladies' Association in the background.*
RIGHT: *Franklin A. Whelan, Mount Vernon's gardener from 1885 to 1927, is shown, sometime after 1902, near the rose beds planted in the upper garden during the Victorian era.*

written by Woodrow Wilson, originally published in *Harper's New Monthly Magazine* in 1896. The collaboration between illustrator and author included extensive discussion about how to depict the main ideas of each article in an engaging and authentic manner. The image of Washington in the upper garden appeared as the frontispiece to the segment "First in Peace," and Pyle proposed the setting to Wilson because the "box-walk at Mount Vernon is now very much as it was in Washington's day" and would "indicate the idea of his Cincinnatus character."[24]

For more than one hundred years, longer than any of the previous garden iterations, the Ladies' Victorian rose garden provided the iconic model for the layout and design of American gardens in the eighteenth-century mode—reinforced through postcards, photographs, and illustrations such as Pyle's, which was hailed as a fitting complement to Wilson's words.[25]

## The 1985 Garden

By the mid-twentieth century, the Ladies were refining their philosophical approach to historic preservation and to how George Washington's Mount Vernon should be presented to the public. Within the upper garden, the Association removed the modern greenhouses, clearing the way for a faithful reconstruction, in 1951, of the brick greenhouse on the footprint of the original structure.[26] This reconstruction, based upon period drawings and historical accounts, marked an important step on the path toward authenticity and helped focus Mount Vernon's period of interpretation on 1799. The change was also instrumental in recognizing that the Victorian rose garden was an outdated vestige of a bygone time. In 1985 both the roses and the lozenge-shaped paths around them (which had been placed inside boundaries almost identical to the two central planting beds of the 1799 garden) were removed.[27]

With the removal of the rose garden, two of the three original large beds—remnants of Washington's eighteenth-century layout—were divided and reconfigured through the creation of many new paths. The new smaller beds held period-appropriate flowers rather than roses, and vegetables were reintroduced to the upper garden (though segregated in the southeast corner). The increase in the numbers of beds and paths created a garden echoing Batty Langley's *New Principles of Gardening* (1728), believed to have been an inspiration for Washington's 1799 garden.[28] The boxwood and the crescent beds were retained, in part because they added surprise and contrast to the garden, two tenets promoted by Langley. They also enabled the Ladies' Association to portray Washington as a creative and informed gardener, familiar with fashionable English practices. Ironically, the layout of the 1799 garden was virtually hidden through these alterations, though the skeleton of its plan was still present. The overgrown boxwood hedges, for example, remained in virtually the same locations as those that had originally bordered the wide gravel routes, but their size now compressed the original 1790s paths. The boxwood's overgrowth radically altered the views and overall design of the garden, creating something vastly different from Washington's ideal.

*Howard Pyle*, Washington in the Garden at Mount Vernon, *1896.*

# Archaeology in the Upper Garden

Prior to the 1985 upper garden restoration, archaeological work in this space was limited to isolated test pits that did not identify earlier garden features. As the boxwood declined, the opportunity for another round of research presented itself. New archaeological testing began in early 2005, and the emerging chronology of paths, including identification of their red clay and gravel eighteenth-century signature, was intriguing enough to warrant a summer of intensive excavation in 2006. This excavation found the first conclusive proof—the 1760s tree plantings and 1770s vegetable beds—to suggest that the upper garden retained a rich history of archaeological features and chronological layering from the eighteenth through the twenty-first centuries. Over the course of five years, roughly 10 percent of the garden was excavated and six phases of the space were identified and mapped.

While the excavations were under way, documentary and comparative research was conducted on the garden books Washington owned, as well as on plans and written descriptions relating to several other formal gardens of the period. These included urban gardens such as those at the Peyton Randolph House in Williamsburg, Virginia, and the William Paca House in Annapolis, Maryland, and Virginia plantation gardens such as those at Prestwould, Westover, Carter's Grove, Mount Pleasant, and Bacon's Castle. Research revolved around one particularly vexing question: Why did many visitors, such as the Reverend John Latta in 1799, only mention seeing flowers, trees, and shrubs when they visited the space, whereas the Mount Vernon gardener's weekly reports from the 1790s almost never mentioned flowers but rather recorded the tending of a variety of vegetables?[29]

What the published garden books and many of the surviving garden plans and descriptions made clear was that large, rectangular beds—like those revealed at Mount Vernon—often were laid out with a combination of flowering plants, fruit trees and shrubs, and vegetables. The vegetables commonly were planted in the interiors of the beds, where there was ample space to set them out in standard rows. The flowering plants, fruit trees, and shrubs could then be arranged in a perimeter bed, often several feet wide, which served as a border running around the plot and enclosing the vegetables. Thus the accounts of the visitors, which focused on the ornamentals, and the gardener's contrasting emphasis on the more utilitarian plants were not contradictory, but likely reflected differing perspectives on the relative importance of the plants found in the garden. These revelations, combined with the strength of the archaeological discoveries, provided the evidence needed to support restoring the garden to its more geometric, simpler plan.

In 2010 the southern portion of the 1985 garden restoration was bulldozed, clearing the way for the seventh iteration of Washington's upper garden. A number of existing features in the northern part of the garden were retained in the new design, as their presence was confirmed by a variety of sources. These include the continued practice of growing fruit trees, both in an orchard laid out in the northwest sector of the space and on espaliers trained against the south side of the greenhouse

*Scale model used for planning the 2010 upper garden restoration.*

*Upper garden, 2012.*

wings and the brick garden wall. The boxwood parterres located in front of the slave quarter wings, flanking the courtyard facing the greenhouse, had been restored in 1998 based on a description by Benjamin Henry Latrobe, who in 1796 recorded seeing "a parterre, chipped and trimmed with infinite care into the form of a richly flourished Fleur de Lis."[30] These familiar elements of the upper garden have been combined with the three recreated large planting beds; the center of each of these is filled with vegetables, bordered by a profusion of flowering plants, fruit trees, and shrubs, and edged with a very low boxwood hedge.

The integration of both flowers and vegetables within the restored upper garden leads to a discussion of Washington's reliance on compromise and practicality—traits that resonate in today's economic and political climate. The renewed emphasis on vegetables in what had been interpreted as a "pleasure garden" fits well with green and locally sourced food themes. Finally, the garden continues to foster a sense of Washington as nurturer but, now, as a nurturer of the beauty of vegetables in simple beds rather than of shaddocks, exotic roses, or mazes of boxwood. And yes, the gardeners intend to keep the boxwood borders trimmed so that they do not overwhelm and hide the wide paths but rather allow sweeping views of the greenhouse and across the expanse of the garden.

All seven iterations of Mount Vernon's upper garden are part of a single continuum of time and activity within the space. Each of them is infused with meaning and symbolism that contribute to our understanding of how successive generations have viewed and interpreted George Washington. Equipped with a more thorough historical knowledge about the garden, we are capable of better understanding the varying themes and stories to which it has contributed over the past two hundred fifty years. Each garden has built upon the one before it to become a representative example of each generation's cultural sense of Washington.

The physical discoveries within the upper garden included classic archaeological features showing the layout of plantings, beds, and paths through time, as well as more ephemeral soil horizons interpreted as evidence of large-scale changes, such as the reorganization of the space carried out during the 1780s and early 1790s. When the system is viewed as a whole, it is possible to pinpoint specific phases of the garden and begin to make sense of how each phase fits into the broader landscape that was crafted outside the garden's walls.

Contrary to what one might expect, the 1799 garden was not consistent with the overall Mount Vernon landscape. In the western part of the garden, where the walls curve in to a point, a cut for a bed was identified running parallel with the primary east-west path. The boundary of this bed was maintained, in almost the same position, from the 1780s until at least the mid-nineteenth century. The relationship of this bed and path suggests that a geometric internal layout was retained in this section of the garden until the digging of the crescent beds created a garden that was more in keeping with the Victorian assumption, which was that Washington would have desired to implement within the upper garden the naturalistic design of his larger picturesque landscape, outside the garden walls.

The picture that emerges from the 2005–10 study suggests that few of the naturalistic principles present in the broader landscape were used in the upper garden. Instead, George Washington's 1799 garden consisted of large squared beds, bordered by wide, straight gravel paths that provided a simple route for navigating the space. This geometric and regular layout facilitated views of the brick greenhouse and the large beds integrated with flowers, fruit trees and shrubs, and vegetables—a profusion of plantings, height, and color visible as one strolled in from the serpentine walk. Mount Vernon's larger, naturalistic landscape was meant to be explored and enjoyed. Washington's upper garden, however, was never brought into this model. It remained a functional workspace, clearly identifiable as man-made, with elements to admire, but not a picturesque pleasure ground.

*New planting bed at western end of upper garden, with seed house in background, 2012.*

# GARDENS AND GROVES

## A Landscape Guide

### Adam T. Erby

## THE VIEWS

Although Mount Vernon's prime location on the Potomac River enabled people to arrive by boat, the vast majority of George Washington's visitors traveled over land—on horseback or by carriage—and entered the estate through what is now commonly called the west gate. There, as visitors turned in between the white gates, they caught their first sight of the house, framed by trees that Washington had carefully cleared to create a picturesque view. The drive ahead curved in and out of the woods, providing tantalizingly brief glimpses as visitors approached the Mansion, which was perfectly situated at the center of Washington's carefully composed "pleasure grounds," the highly cultivated, ornamental spaces created for the enjoyment of his guests.[1]

The long, narrow clearing from the west gate to the Mansion offered the estate's primary and most impressive "visto," staked out by Washington himself in 1785 and stretching on axis with the Mansion's front door. He designed this clearing to provide visitors with a commanding view of the house from seven-tenths of a mile away and so heighten their anticipation of the estate they would encounter. He also laid out several other secondary vistas to focus visitors' sight lines on the most picturesque prospects on his property. Each vista was cleared and maintained by his

*View toward Mansion from west gate, 2014.*

enslaved workers, who cleared brush from tree lines and planted additional varieties of trees to create richly textured scenes.

The most highly anticipated view at Mount Vernon was the breathtaking panorama, from the Mansion piazza, of the Potomac and the Maryland shore beyond. About this sight the British architect Benjamin Henry Latrobe wrote, "Towards the East of the Mansion Nature has lavished its magnificence, nor has Art interfered but to exhibit her to advantage."[2] Latrobe understood that the scene before him was not entirely natural but was the result of a carefully managed design.

To create the view, Washington instructed his workers to grade the east lawn at its center in order to reveal more of the river. This work provided a gentle sweep at the center of the lawn, capped on either side by a small knoll. Below the grassy depression, Washington cut a vista in the trees at the riverbank, exposing still more water to the eye. He also built a ha-ha, or ditch with a brick wall, just below the crest of the hill and not visible from the piazza. Besides keeping livestock from wandering onto the Mansion grounds, the ha-ha fostered the illusion that the manicured lawn continued toward the river. Farther down the slope was what English landscape designers called a hanging wood—a cluster of neatly trimmed trees that were never allowed to grow tall enough to obscure the view of the Potomac. In order to enhance the panorama still further, Washington broke with rules of classical architecture, using thin, square columns on the piazza rather than perfectly proportioned round ones.[3]

ABOVE: *Fragment of 18th-century iron scythe blade, found in archaeological excavation at Mount Vernon.* RIGHT: *Benjamin Henry Latrobe,* View to the North from the Lawn at Mount Vernon, *1796.*

North from the Lawn at Mount Vernon.

A                    B                    BL July 5. 1796.

ABOVE: *East facade of Mansion in the early morning, 2014.* RIGHT: *Benjamin Henry Latrobe,* View of Mount Vernon with the Washington Family on the Piazza, *1796.*

Benjamin Henry Latrobe nat. del.

ABOVE: *Potomac River and Maryland shore from piazza, 2012. The 18th-century swamp chestnut oak tree seen here fell in 2014.* RIGHT: *Detail of Latrobe's* View of Mount Vernon with the Washington Family on the Piazza, *showing George and Martha (seated), Eleanor (Nelly) Parke Custis and her dog Frisk, and an unidentified small boy. The man looking through the spyglass may be Latrobe.*

# BOWLING GREEN

George Washington devised, as the central element of his landscape composition, a level, well-manicured lawn, admiringly described by one French nobleman as "a kind of courtyard with a green carpet."[4] While modern visitors may be accustomed to such wide expanses of evenly trimmed grass, eighteenth-century lawns were expensive to plant and required extensive labor to maintain. After leveling the ground for the guitar-shaped bowling green west of the Mansion, Washington sought enough English or Goose grass seed "as would sow five acres," noting that "the kind I want is that which affords the best turf for walks and lawns."[5] Clement Biddle, his purchasing agent in Philadelphia, had difficulty procuring such lawn seed, as there was little demand for ornamental grass in America.[6]

Once grass was planted, keeping it cut was not nearly as simple as getting out a lawnmower. The day before a grass cutting, gardeners smoothed the ground with a large stone roller to create an even surface for cutting. The next day, they cut the grass by swinging the blade of a freshly sharpened scythe back and forth in a repetitive motion. Maintaining an even surface and uniform height required skill, and only the most experienced gardeners were allowed to perform this task. As they worked their way across the bowling green, they repeatedly paused to sharpen their blades with stones carried on their belts.[7]

To tie together the different elements of his landscape composition, Washington laid out a "serpentine path" hugging the contours of the bowling green. This gently curving gravel walkway guided visitors through Mount Vernon's pleasure grounds, revealing carefully arranged scenes around every bend. The S-curves of the serpentine path gave the landscape a more natural appearance, strongly contrasting with the straight, formal walks of most eighteenth-century American landscapes. Along the path, Washington planted forest trees, which framed the views and offered welcome shade, protecting visitors from the powerful Virginia sun. These trees were much more densely planted during Washington's time, prompting at least one visitor to marvel at what seemed to him a "thousand kinds of trees, plants, and bushes" encountered along the bowling green.[8]

Walking west from the Mansion along the serpentine path, Washington's guests first encountered a "shrubbery" on either side of the bowling green, where flowering bushes created bursts of color. At the bend of the path along the northern side of the green, a pair of gates came into view, leading to the upper garden and greenhouse. Farther along, visitors encountered Washington's "pine labyrinths," which were so thickly planted with evergreens that the sun barely penetrated. A pathway snaking through each labyrinth allowed visitors to explore these spaces before emerging back onto the serpentine walk as it opened onto the bowling green, with the sight of the Mansion on one side and the vista to the west gate on the other.[9]

LEFT: *Bowling green and Mansion from the west, 2012.* ABOVE: *Stone garden roller used at Mount Vernon in the 18th century.*

**LEFT:** West Front of Mount Vernon, *from about 1787–92 and attributed to Edward Savage, shows the Washington family strolling across the bowling green.* **ABOVE:** *Serpentine path, fall 2012.*

# UPPER GARDEN

After George Washington's 1785 landscape alterations, the upper garden served as a formal space for his guests' enjoyment. Filled with a rich variety of plants in the highest state of cultivation, it showcased his prowess as a gentleman farmer. The design was rigidly symmetrical, offering a pleasing contrast to the curved lines of the bowling green. The centerpiece of the garden was the large brick greenhouse where Washington nurtured tropical and semitropical plants. The garden proper was divided into six planting beds by wide pathways of gravel and packed clay, directing visitors' steps as they walked. During the warmer months, the gardener took the tropical plants out of the greenhouse and placed them around the garden, where they could receive direct sunlight and rain.[10]

At the center of each of the three main planting beds Washington sowed rows of vegetables and fruit trees for household use. To highlight the beauty of the practical plantings inside, each bed was "bordered with dwarf box wood interspersed with ornamental flowering shrubs with ornamental trees around the exterior of the inclosure."[11] Combining an aesthetically pleasing landscape with food production, these planting beds demonstrated the beauty of domestic agriculture. Washington seems to have highlighted America's Revolutionary War alliance with the French, installing in one of the planting beds a boxwood parterre "chipped and trimmed with infinite care into the form of a richly flourished Fleur de Lis."[12] Against the perimeter of the brick wall he planted espaliered fruit trees. Painstakingly pruned and trained to grow flat against the wall, such plants showed that Washington possessed both the financial resources and the labor force to maintain them.

Because the upper garden was the highlight of any visitor's tour of Mount Vernon's pleasure grounds, many commented on what they saw there. In 1799 a Pennsylvania clergyman, the Reverend John Latta, remarked, "The garden is very handsomely laid out in squares and flower knots, and contains a great variety of tree[s], flower[s] and plants of foreign growth collected from almost every part of the world."[13] When the Polish nobleman Julian Ursyn Niemcewicz visited, in 1798, he noticed the more practical plantings inside, observing "all the vegetables for the kitchen, Corrents, Rasberys, Strawberys, Gusberys, [and] quantities of peaches and cherries."[14]

*Flower border surrounding rows of vegetables, with greenhouse in background, 2013.*

LEFT: *Dwarf boxwood edging a floral border in one of the upper garden's new large beds, 2013.* ABOVE: *Great double daisy, from George Washington's copy of William Curtis's* Botanical Magazine *(1794).*

# GREENHOUSE AND
# SLAVE QUARTER

The focal point of the upper garden was a substantial greenhouse. In this heated building, George Washington cultivated delicate tropical and semitropical plants that could not withstand cold Virginia winters. In addition to providing lemons, limes, and oranges for Mrs. Washington's table, the greenhouse served as a gallery for exhibiting rare and unusual plants imported from around the globe, including aloe vera from North Africa and sago palm from the East Indies.

When Washington began planning the greenhouse, in 1784, there were very few such structures in North America and none near Mount Vernon. Although he had seen several examples in his travels, he was unfamiliar with the mechanics of a system that generated radiant heat from a series of flues under the floor. Therefore, he wrote his trusted aide Colonel Tench Tilghman, seeking details of Margaret Tilghman Carroll's greenhouse outside Baltimore.[15] Combining these details with his recollections and observations, Washington designed his own greenhouse, completing construction of the main block in the summer of 1787.[16]

LEFT: *Ruined walls of slave quarter, circa 1889.* RIGHT: *Upper garden, greenhouse, and one slave quarter wing, 2012.*

The building was designed to be both beautiful and functional; almost every element of it had a practical purpose. The thick brick walls provided a pleasing contrast to the white woodwork; they also retained heat and insulated the building. The five large triple-sash windows added a vertical thrust to the design, but their primary purpose was to provide maximum exposure to sunlight from the south. The sashes could be opened at both top and bottom to promote air circulation. The pair of wide, low wings, added in 1792, balanced the strong verticality of the central structure and housed slaves who lived at the Mansion House Farm.

Washington's plan to add the two wings dates to about 1785, appearing in his sketch of the greenhouse complex. Construction of the wings was in full swing in 1792, when the president corresponded with his farm manager and nephew, George Augustine Washington, about the project.[17] Each wing contained two rooms, with a single fireplace in each. In these rooms, Washington added "berths"—bunks similar to those that might have been found in a military encampment. There were likely ten bunks in every room, and each could have slept two slaves. Thus as many as eighty of the eighty-seven slaves on the farm could have lodged in the greenhouse slave quarter. In the central block there was also a shop where Washington's trusted slave Billy Lee made and repaired shoes for the many slaves on the plantation. Injuries kept Lee from doing more active work.[18]

The greenhouse complex was one of the most socially divided spaces at Mount Vernon. To the south, the central room for tropical plants opened onto the refined upper garden, designed to be enjoyed by the Washingtons and their guests. To the north, the two wings for enslaved workers opened onto a service lane. The greenhouse burned in 1835, but luckily its appearance had been recorded in two early nineteenth-century insurance documents.[19] Using these sketches and extensive archaeological evidence, the Mount Vernon Ladies' Association reconstructed the building in 1951 on its original foundations.

ABOVE: *Gravel recovered in upper garden excavation, originally hauled up from Potomac River by slaves.*
TOP RIGHT: *Greenhouse and slave quarter, drawn by Lewis M. Rivalain in 1803 for the Mutual Assurance Society of Virginia.* BOTTOM RIGHT: *George Washington's circa 1785 drawing for possible layout of greenhouse and slave quarter wings.*

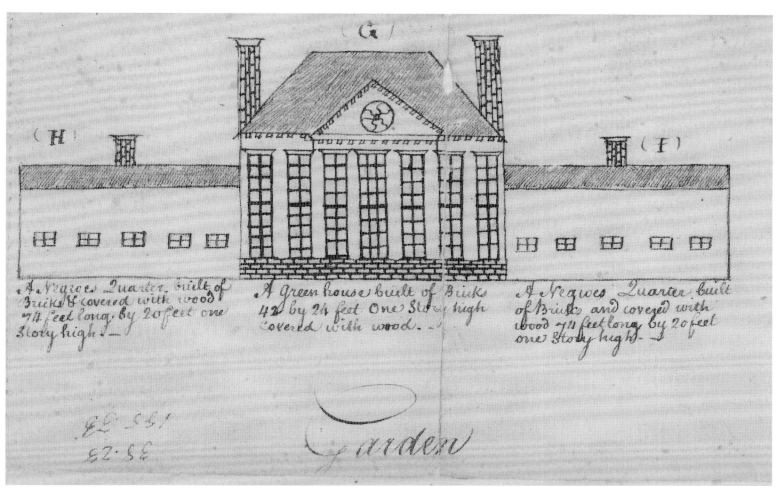

(G)

(H)                                                                (I)

A Negroes Quarter built of Bricks & covered with wood 74 feet long by 20 feet one Story high —

A Green house built of Bricks 42 by 24 feet One Story high Covered with wood. —

A Negroes Quarter built of Bricks and covered with wood 74 feet long by 20 feet one Story high —

Garden

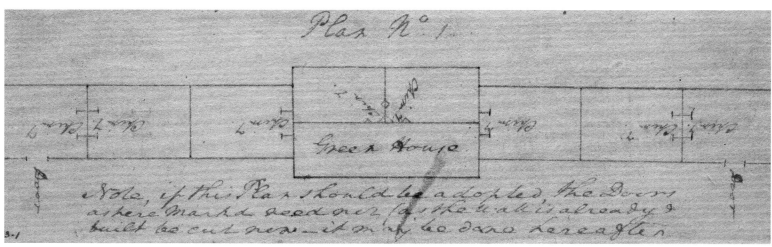

Plan N°. 1.

Green House

Note, if this Plan should be adopted, the Doors as here marked need not (as the wall is already built be cut now it may be done hereafter

CENTURY PLANT AND LEMON-TREE.

**ABOVE:** *Visitors admire Mount Vernon's century plant and lemon tree, circa 1859.*
**RIGHT:** *Interior of greenhouse, 1987.*

ABOVE: *The slave quarter opened onto a service lane behind the greenhouse.* RIGHT: *Interior of women's quarter, as installed in 2010.*

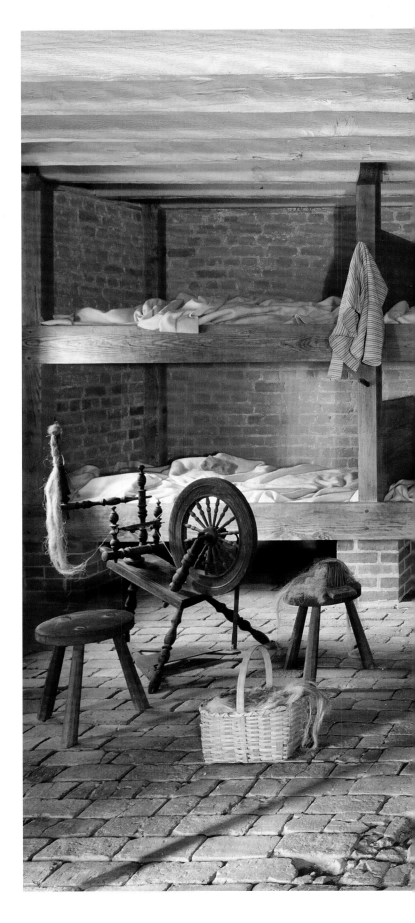

# LOWER GARDEN

Before grocery stores and farmers' markets, kitchen gardens were, as one 1778 gardening manual observed, "a necessary support of life."[20] In the eighteenth century, most homes maintained such gardens to provide produce that supplemented the rest of the diet. Mount Vernon's lower garden has been continuously cultivated for the production of vegetables, fruits, and herbs since 1760. "There is an immense, extremely well-cultivated garden behind the right wing," a visitor in 1782 noted. "The choicest fruits in the country are to be found there."[21] While the lower garden was not intended for pleasure, the gate off the bowling green may have enticed visitors to peek inside.[22] The garden supplied such essentials for the Washington family table as lettuce, broccoli, cabbage, and cauliflower as well as herbs such as dill and chives.

Set into the side of a hill sloping off to the south of the bowling green, the lower garden's southern exposure provides the best direct sunlight on the estate, facilitating longer growing seasons for this vital plot of land. Early in Washington's ownership of Mount Vernon, he had his slaves divide this space into two level terraces that could be laid out in squares and rows of fruits and vegetables. Gardeners he hired to superintend estate maintenance were expected to be skilled kitchen gardeners. During his presidential years in New York and Philadelphia, he required the gardener to send him weekly reports specifying the work done and the fruits and vegetables harvested.

Meals served by the Washingtons typically included fruits and vegetables. As food preparation was overseen by Martha Washington, she was also directly involved with kitchen garden operations. She would have told the hired gardener what kinds of produce the enslaved cooks would need to make meals for the Mansion's table. Her authority in this regard is often difficult to discern in the documentary record, because these were among the daily chores of running a household, rarely commented upon. Occasionally, however, she sent instructions home for the gardener, as in one 1792 letter to her niece Fanny Bassett Washington, advising her to "impress it on the gardener to have every thing in his garden that will be ne[ce]ssary in the House keeping way—as vegetable is the best part of our living in the country."[23]

Mount Vernon's many guests were often surprised by the types and varieties of fruits and vegetables served there. When visiting in June 1797, the Massachusetts preacher Amariah Frost "viewed the garden and walks, which are very elegant, abounding with many curiosities, Fig trees, raisins, limes, oranges, etc., large English mulberries, artichokes, etc." That afternoon, he dined with the Washington family and was impressed by the food, including "a small roasted pigg, boiled leg of lamb, roasted fowls, [and] beef" as well as the vegetables that were in season, including "peas, lettuce, cucumbers, artichokes, etc."[24]

*As laid out in 1936 and seen here in 2012, Mount Vernon's lower garden contains many small planting beds. The Washingtons' 18th-century kitchen garden likely contained simple rows of plants rather than geometrically arranged beds.*

**LEFT:** *Herbs, cabbages, and espaliered fruit trees in the lower garden, 2012. The brick wall absorbs and radiates heat, keeping espaliered trees warm and extending their growing season.*
**ABOVE:** *Charles Willson Peale's 1772 portrait miniature of Martha Washington.*

# BOTANICAL GARDEN

Off the north lane, between the spinning house and the upper garden brick wall, George Washington fenced in a small parcel to serve as a 'Botanick,' or experimental garden, where he could test new plants before introducing them in other parts of the estate. He wrote in 1793 that his intention for this plot "was to receive such things as required but a small space for their cultivation."[25] The vast majority of gardening manuals then available in America were written by British authors and specific to growing conditions in Great Britain. So Washington used his "little garden" to see how plants might fare in the harsher Virginia climate. The botanical garden's proximity to the Mansion enabled him and his gardeners to monitor the plantings closely.

Many of the seeds planted in the botanical garden were gifts to the general from friends or acquaintances. In the summer of 1785, he received one of his most interesting such gifts, Chinese seeds from his friends Dr. James Craik and the Alexandria merchant Thomas Porter. The seeds were accompanied by a note with the Chinese names spelled phonetically for the plants "which are accompanied by characters or hierogliphics [*sic*]." These plants included "Be yack fa" and "Si fu he Tons." The seeds were likely some of the first to arrive in the United States directly from China after trade opened between the two countries in 1783. Unfortunately, the seeds must have been too old, for they did not succeed.[26]

Washington's experiments with Guinea grass, a native African species, illustrate his careful observations of and involvement with the botanical garden. In June 1785, his nephew George Augustine Washington returned from Barbados with samples of various seeds, including Guinea grass, for the general to experiment with at Mount Vernon. The two men thought this new variety might produce an excellent hay crop. In November, Washington covered the guinea grass to protect it from the frost but left six rows uncovered "to try the effect of the Winters frosts & snows upon it."[27] Apparently, none of the grass survived the winter, but Washington was eager to try to cultivate more, as he later observed that the "growth is rapid—drought has no effect on it—and the quantity it yields is astonishing."[28]

*George Washington's botanical garden, 2012.*

# OUTBUILDINGS

One eighteenth-century visitor to Virginia observed that plantations "Shew Like little villages, for having Kitchens, Dayry houses, Barns, Stables, Store houses, and some of them 2 or 3 Negro Quarters."[29] Each of these small villages functioned as the working center of its plantation, providing foodstuffs, storage, and housing for its many residents, both enslaved and free. Close proximity to the master's house facilitated the watchful eye of the plantation owner—guarding against theft and overseeing the labor force.[30]

In 1775 Washington razed Mount Vernon's existing outbuildings, which stood too close to his new additions to the Mansion. He replaced those with structures situated in a neat, symmetrical arrangement along the north and south lanes. This placement allowed him to minimize their visibility from the house and pleasure grounds. To the east, groves of trees shielded the view of the outbuildings from the Mansion, while to the west, the brick garden walls blocked glimpses of messy processes such as smoking meat, blacksmithing, washing laundry, and mucking out horse stalls.[31]

Each work lane was fenced around its perimeter so that Washington and his white employees could more carefully monitor who entered and left these areas, which often contained valuable items. Along the north lane were the gardener's house, the salt house (for salt and fishing gear), the spinning house (for flax and wool processing and storage), and the blacksmith's shop. Washington placed the storehouse at the entrance to the south lane, so that it would be visible from the Mansion and thus help prevent the theft of tools, powder for shot, clothing and blankets for the slaves, and other plantation goods. This lane then passed by the smokehouse, washhouse, dung (fertilizer) repository, and the stable yard.

The exteriors of the Mansion and the outbuildings are made of wood, with those facing the carriage circle in front of the house finished to look like stone. First, long pine boards were grooved and beveled to create the appearance of masonry blocks. The boards were then varnished and painted, and fine sand was thrown onto the wet paint, giving the surface a rough texture. With an eye to both economy and appearance, Washington used this process, called "rustication," only on the sides of outbuildings visible from the house. The rest of the buildings along the north and south lanes were painted the same color, creating a harmonious effect.

*Outbuildings line the south lane
leading to the Mansion circle, 2007.*

ABOVE: *View toward Mansion from lower garden, 2007.* RIGHT: *A gate at the end of the north lane limited access to the area immediately in front of the Mansion.*

Supposing the dot at A to be the highest part of the hill in front of the House, & the black line from D to C by A the natural shape of the hill (or fall of the hill) the pricked line may be a good direction for the walk, in order to prevent its being too serpentine or crooked — this, in some places, will come in upon the level (or that which is nearly so) of the hill — as at 1, 2, 3 — and in others as at 5, 6, 7 & 8. will be below the declivity, & require filling up in order to bring the whole to a level, which is to be effected by the earth which may be taken from 1, 2, 3 ——

There are two reasons for doing it in this manner — the one is, to prevent the walk from being too serpentine & crooked (as the black line) — and the second is, that the hill below the walk may be more of a sameness — otherwise it wd. descend very suddenly in some places and very gradually in others. —

You will observe that this walk is not to be laid out, or worked by a line — the whole of it is serpentine, which I am particular in mentioning because by the expression in your letter of Zig-Zag, you had an idea that it was to be laid out by line 20 or 30 feet or yards (as the hill would admit) one way then angling & as far as it would go strait another in the followg. manr.

It is not my wish to have it very serpentine nor would I have it quite strait if I could — a little curving and meandering would be my choice

# THE LOST DEER PARK

Following British aristocratic practice, George Washington in 1785 fenced off eighteen acres on the east slope, between the Mansion and the Potomac River, to be used as "a paddock for deer," or deer park.[32] Originating in the Middle Ages, deer parks initially served as large hunting preserves for kings and nobles. While retaining elite associations, Washington's deer park served a purely picturesque function, providing his guests with the delightful spectacle of seemingly wild deer roaming through parkland.[33]

In August 1785, Washington wrote friends both home and abroad, seeking English deer in addition to the common American variety. His good friend Benjamin Ogle maintained a park stocked with English deer at Bell-Air, his plantation near Annapolis. When Washington's letter reached Ogle, he "immediately endeavour'd to get" several deer for the general, but he found them "too forward." He explained to Washington that "unless they are caught within ten days [of birth] its [sic] as difficult [to catch fawns] as to catch the old ones."[34]

The following summer, Ogle sent six English fawns captured on his plantation, providing Washington with an initial stock.[35] In addition, Washington's old friend and neighbor George William Fairfax sent from Great Britain a "buck & doe of the best English deer." Washington later commented that the English deer are "very distinguishable by the darkness of their colour, and their horns." When writing Fairfax about his deer park in 1786, he alluded to its role in helping him "to be a participator of the tranquility and rural amusements" that he so eagerly sought after the Revolutionary War.[36]

Although British landscape manuals advised paddock owners not to approach the animals, so that they would remain wild, at least some of Washington's deer were tame. Sadly, his park declined while he was away serving as president, and deer broke through the surrounding picket fence. From that point on, some deer continued to roam the estate and were treated almost as family pets. In 1794 Washington reported that the "Gardener complains of the injury which the shrubs (even in the yard) sustain from the Deer. I am at a loss therefore in determining whether to give up the Shrubs or the Deer!"[37]

Washington was protective of his deer even after they were no longer confined to the park, and he prohibited locals from hunting these animals on the estate. Despite this precaution, in 1793 his prized black buck was killed by a hunter, and Washington apparently believed that the perpetrator was his neighbor Richard Chichester.[38] When Chichester learned of his supposed crime, he fired off an indignant letter, claiming that he had not killed the deer, insisting instead that "A certain Charles Dodson . . . told me himself that he kill'd a large deer of that Colour just about the time I heard of the loss of Yours."[39] Washington had previously warned Chichester not to hunt on Mount Vernon land and so may not have been convinced of the man's innocence.

*George Washington's 1798 drawing of a ha-ha wall to replace the deer park.*

LEFT: East Front of Mount Vernon, *circa 1787–92.*
*Attributed to Edward Savage, this painting includes*
*the only known view of Washington's deer park, which*
*was located on the slope below the east lawn.* ABOVE:
Black Buck, *a silk-embroidered picture of circa 1793–95*
*attributed to Martha Washington.* OVERLEAF: *East slope*
*below Mansion, site of the lost deer park, 2010.*

*James Peller Malcolm's watercolor-and-ink drawing of* Woodlands, the Seat of W. Hamilton, Esq., from the Bridge at Grey's Ferry, *circa 1792.*

# Plants from William Hamilton, March 1792

In early 1792, George Washington asked his friend William Hamilton to send him a number of unusual plants. A wealthy amateur botanist and patron of the arts, Hamilton lived at The Woodlands, a three-hundred-acre estate with a neoclassical villa, along the banks of the Schuylkill River just south of Philadelphia. On his grounds and in his greenhouse, Hamilton cultivated approximately ten thousand species of plants, including trees and shrubs. Washington received the plants listed below at the president's house in Philadelphia on March 19 and sent them to Mount Vernon, together with a larger group of plants he had purchased that same month from John Bartram's nursery, also located south of Philadelphia.[1]

| No. | Plant | Description | Number of plants |
|---|---|---|---|
| 1 | Spanish chestnut | bears very large Fruit | 2 |
| 2 | Bladder Senna | with yellow Flowers (grows 10 or 12 feet high) | |
| 3 | Laburnum | call'd Ebony of the alps (12 or 15 feet high) | 4 |
| 4 | Roan tree, or Mountain ash | bears beautiful clusters of red fruit | 4 |
| 5 | Flowering Raspberry | | 8 |
| 6 | Twice bearing Raspberry | (the fruit excellent) | 12 |
| 7 | Pyracantha, or Evergreen Thorn | | 2 |
| 8 | white flowering Lilac | | 6 |
| 9 | Manna ash from Italy | | 2 |
| 10 | Junipers | | 2 |
| 11 | Willow with variegated leaves | | 2 |
| 12 | Paper Mulberry of Japan | | 4 |
| 13 | English white Thorn | the sort used for hedges | 1 |
| 14 | St Peters wort | (grows 3 or 4 feet high) | 4 |
| 15 | Hypericum: shrub St Johns wort | (4 feet high) | 6 |
| 16 | Spirea frutex | | 4 |
| 17 | Dwarf Syringa, or Mock orange | with double flowers | 4 |
| 18 | Rose Acacia | | 15 |
| 19 | Double flowering Almonds | | 3 |
| 20 | Willow with Bay leaves | | 2 |
| 21 | English Laurel | | 1 |

| No. | Plant | Description | Number of plants |
|---|---|---|---|
| 22 | Spanish broom, & white broom | 1 plant of each | 2 |
| 23 | Double flowering Bramble | | 5 |
| 24 | Common Broom | | 24 |
| 25 | Dwarf American Laurel | | 12 |
| 26 | Rhododendron or Mountain Rose Laurel | | 4 |
| | *Cuttings* | | |
| 27 | True Osier, or Basket willow | | |
| 28 | Flowering, or Palm Do [willow] | | |
| 29 | Bay leafed Do [willow] | | |
| 30 | Variegated Do [willow] | | 3 |

# Plants from John Bartram's Nursery, March 1792

In March 1792, George Washington purchased the plants listed below from William Bartram—son of the Pennsylvania botanist John Bartram—who operated a commercial nursery south of Philadelphia. The nursery was on the banks of the Schuylkill River, not far from William Hamilton's Woodlands estate.[2] The list itemizes a variety of ornamental plants, including trees and shrubs, that Washington sent to Mount Vernon to be placed in oval beds on either side of the bowling green.[3] Each specimen was marked with a wooden stake inscribed with a number corresponding to its entry on the list; these markings enabled Washington's gardener to identify the plants quickly.[4] William Bartram listed both the Latin and common names of each plant, provided a florid description of its key features, and noted its expected height. (Heights are not included here.)

Founded by John Bartram, the nursery gained international renown for the rare specimens it offered. The elder Bartram and his two sons sought native plants on expeditions throughout eastern North America. Bringing their finds back to Philadelphia, they studied and propagated each species and slowly built up a large collection of indigenous plants. They sold items both domestically and abroad, fueling a desire among wealthy European gardeners for exciting new plants from North America. The business continued to be called John Bartram's nursery after his death in 1777.

| No. | Plant | Description | Common name(s) | Number of plants |
|---|---|---|---|---|
| 1 | Rhododendron maximum | Evergreen, large maximum rose coloured blossoms | "Mountain laurel," great laurel, rosebay | 2 |
| 2 | Ulex europeus | Embellished with sweet scented flowers, of a fine yellow colour | Furze | 2 |
| 3 | Hypericum kalmianum | Profusely garnished with fine Gold coloured blossoms | "Shrub St. John's wort" | 2 |
| 4 | H[ypericum] Angustifolium | Evergreen; adorned with fine yellow flowers | | 3 |
| 5 | Taxus procumbens | Evergreen; of a splendid full green throughout the year—red berries | Yew | 1 |
| 6 | Buxus aureis [aureus] | Elegant, call'd gilded box | | 1 |
| 7 | Daphne mezerium [mezereum] | An early flowering sweet scented little shrub | Mezereon, paradise plant | 2 |
| 8 | Calycanthus floridus | Odoriferous, its blossoms scented like the Pine apple | "Sweet Shrub of Carolina," Carolina allspice | 5 |
| 9 | Berberis canadensis | Berries of a perfect coral red | Barberry | 3 |

| No. | Plant | Description | Common name(s) | Number of plants |
|---|---|---|---|---|
| 10 | *Æsculus hippocastanum* | A magnificent flowering & shady Tree | Horse chestnut | 2 |
| 11 | *Evonimus atrapurpurous [Euonymus atropurpureus]* | Its fruit of a bright crimson in the Autumn | (burning bush) | 3 |
| 12 | *Fothergilla gardeni[i]* | Early in blossom; flowers in spikes, white & delicate | Dwarf fothergilla, dwarf witchalder | 6 |
| 13 | *Franklinia alatamaha* | Flowers large, white & fragrant— native of Georgia | Franklin tree | 1 |
| 14 | *Baccharis [prob. Baccharis halimifolia]* | In autumn silvered over with white silky down | prob. groundsel tree | 3 |
| 15 | *Laurus estivalis [aestivalis]* | Aromatic & beautified with coral red berries | Bay tree | 1 |
| 16 | *Kalmia angustifolia (with the Gaultheria [procumbens], or mountain tea [wintergreen])* | Evergreen; garnished with crimson speckled flowers | "Thyme leav'd Kalmia," lambkill, sheep laurel | |
| 17 | *Ilex angustifolia* | Evergreen, new | Holly | 1 |
| 18 | *Dirca palustris* | Early in bloom; singular—(call'd Leather wood) | "Leather Bark" | 2 |
| 19 | *Thuja occidentalis* | A handsome evergreen Tree; beautiful folliage, & odoriferous | American arborvitae, white cedar | 4 |
| 20 | *Zanthorhiza apiifolia [Xanthorhiza simplicissima]* | Singular flowers early: its root affords a splendid transparent yellow dye | (call'd Yellow root, in Carola) | 6 |
| 21 | *Jeffersonia egrilla* | Foliage of deep splendid green, & embellished with a delicate plumage of white flowers | (call'd Iron wood) | 1 |
| 22 | *Magnolia tripetala* | Foliage ample, expansive & light, plumed with large white flowers, which are succeeded by large crimson strobile | "Umbrella Tree" | 1 |
| 23 | *Magnolia acuminata* | Erect with a pyramidal head, the dry strobile odoriferous | "Cucumber Tree" | 1 |
| 24 | *Halesia tetraptera [or carolina]* | The flowers abundant, white, of the shape of little bells | Carolina silverbell | 1 |
| 25 | *Viburnum opulifolium* | of singular beauty in flower and fruit | | 1 |

Catalogue of Trees, Shrubs & Plants, of Ino Bartram.

33877

| | Plants | feet high | |
|---|---|---|---|

1. Rhododendron maximum — 2. grow from 5 to 10. Leaves large rose coloured blossoms.

2. Ulex europeus E — 2. — 3 to 4. Embellished with sweet scented flowers of a fine yellow colour.

3. Hypericum kalmianum — 2. — 3 to 4. Profusely garnished with fine gold coloured blossoms. —

4. H. Angustifolium 3. — 3 to 6. Evergreen, adorned with fine yellow flowers.

5. Taxus procumbens — 1. — 3 to 6. Evergreen, of a splendid full green throughout the year — red berries.

6. Buxus aureis E — 1. — 3 to 10. Elegant, call'd gilded box.

7. Daphne mezerium E — 2. — 1 to 3. an early flowering sweet scented little Shrub. —

8. Calycanthus floridus — 5. — 4 to 8. Odoriferous, its blossoms scented like the Pine apple. —

9. Berberis canadensis — 3. — 2 to 4. Berries of a perfect candied

10. Aesculus hippocastanum — 2. — 20, 40 to 80. A magnificent flowering & Shady Tree. —

11. Evonimus atropurpurea 3. — 6 to 8. Its fruit of a bright crimson in the autumn (burning bush).

12. Fothergilla gardoni — 6. — 2 to 4. early in blossom; flowers in Spikes, white & delicate.

13. Franklinia alatamaha 1. — 3, 15 to 20. Flowers large, white & fragrant — native of Georgia. —

14. Baccharis — 3. — 4 to 6. In autumn filvered over with white silky down

15. Laurus estivalis — 1. — 5 to 8. Aromatic & beautified with coraleed berries. —

16. Kalmia angustifolia with the } 1 to 2. Evergreen, garnished Gaultheria, or mountain tea } with crimson speckled flowers.

17. Ilex angustifolia — 1. — 3 to 6. Evergreen, new.

18. Dirca palustris — 2. — 2 to 3. early in bloom; singular — (call'd Leather wood).

19. Thuya occidentalis — 4. — 15, 30 to 40. A handsome evergreen Tree; beautiful foliage, & odoriferous.

20. Xanthorhiza apiifolia — 6. — 1 to 3. Singular flowers early, its root affords a splendid transparent yellow dye call'd yellow root, in Carolina.

21. Jeffersonia egritia — 4. — 4 to 10. Foliage deep splendid green, & embellished with a delicate plumage of white flowers, call'd Iron wood.

22. Magnolia tripetala — 1. — 8 to 15. Foliage ample, expansive & light, plumed with large white flowers, which are succeeded by large crimson strobile. —

23. Magnolia acuminata — 1. — 30, 80 to 100. Erect with a pyramidal head, the dry strobile odoriferous.

24. Halesia tetraptera — 1. — 4, 10, to 15. the flowers abundant, white, of the shape of little bells.

*First page of "Catalogue of Trees, Shrubs & Plants of Jno Bartram—March 1792."*

| No. | Plant | Description | Common name(s) | Number of plants |
|-----|-------|-------------|----------------|------------------|
| 26 | *Viburnum Arboreum* | very shewy in flower. fruit eatable | | 2 |
| 27 | *Viburnum Alnifolium* [*Viburnum lantanoides*] | handsome flowering shrub | Hobble bush | 2 |
| 28 | *Cupressus disticha* | stature majestic, foliage most delicate, wood of a fine yellow colour, odoriferious & incorruptible | "Bald Cyprus" | 1 |
| 29 | *Sorbus sativa* [*prob. Sorbus domestica*] | Its fruit pear & apple shaped, as large & well tasted when mellow | prob. service tree | 1 |
| 30 | *Carpinus ostrya* | handsome form, dress becoming, fruit singular | (Hop tree) "Horn Beam" | 3 |
| 31 | *Sorbus aucuparia* | Foliage elegant, embellished with umbells of coral red berries | European mountain ash | 2 |
| 32 | *Acer striatum* [*Acer pensylvanicum*] | singularly beautiful; the younger branches inscribed with silvery lines, or scrawls, on a dark purpleish green ground | Striped maple, moosewood | 1 |
| 33 | *Acer glaucum* [*Acer saccharinum*] | beautiful foliage. spreading & shady | (Silver-leaf'd Maple) | 2 |
| 34 | *Acer sacharinum* [*Acer saccharum*] | A stately Tree, in his native forests | (Sugar Maple) | 1 |
| 35 | *Acer platanoides* | graceful stature, full of asscending branches, foliage & flower elegant, casts a grateful shade on the Lawn | Norway maple | 2 |
| 36 | *Stewartia malachodendron* | Floriferous, the flowers large & white embellished with a large tuft of black or purple threads in their centre | Silky stewartia or stuartia | 4 |
| 37 | *Clethra alnifolia* | Flowers abundant in spikes, exceedingly sweet scented | "Clethra," sweet pepperbush | 1 |
| 38 | *Styrax grandifolium* | a most charming flowering shrub, blossoms snow white & of the most grateful scent | (call'd Snow-drop tree), Snowbell, storax | 1 |
| 39 | *Philadelphus coronarius* | a sweet flowering shrub | (call'd a Mock Orange) | 2 |
| 40 | *Philadelphus inodorus* | his robe a silvery flower'd mantle | | 1 |

| No. | Plant | Description | Common name(s) | Number of plants |
|-----|-------|-------------|----------------|------------------|
| 41 | *Pinus Strobus* | Magnificent! he presides in the evergreen Groves | (white pine) | 6 |
| 42 | *Pinus communis* | a stately tree, foliage of a Seagreen colour, & exhibits a good appearance whilst young | (Scotch Fir) | 2 |
| 43 | *Pinus Larix* | elegant figure & foliage | "Larch Tree" | 1 |
| 44 | *Thuja orientalis* | Foliage pleasing | Oriental arborvitae | 1 |
| 45 | *Robinia villosa* | a gay shrub, enrobed with plumed leaves & roseat flowers | "Peach Blossom Acacia" | 4 |
| 46 | *Pinus balsamea* [*Abies balsamea*] | a tree of pleasing figure, delicate foliage, evergreen, & affords fragrant & medicinal balsam | (Balm of Gilead Fir) | 6 |
| 47 | *Pinus abies virginiana* | A Stately evergreen Tree, his foliage of delicate appearance; the wood useful and durable, & of great value | (Hemlock Spruce) | 5 |
| 48 | *Cornus mascula* [or *mas*] | flowers early, the fruit oblong of the size of a plum, of a fine crimson colour, and wholsome pleasant eating | Cornelian cherry | 1 |
| 49 | *Prunus cerasus, flore roseo* | more or less according to the stock; a very beautiful flowering tree, its blushing blossoms double | (double flowering cherry) | 1 |
| 50 | *Prunus maritima* | flowers early, fruit of a dark purple sweet & pleasant eating | "Beach or Sea-side-Plumb" | 1 |
| 51 | *Prunus missisipi* | Fruit of the largest size, oval; of a perfect deep crimson colour, possesses an agreeable taste, & affords an animating marmolade | "Crimson Plumb" | 1 |
| 52 | *Prunus chicasa* | Early flowering, very fruitful; the fruit nearly round, cleft, red, purple, yellow, of an inticing look, most agreeable taste & wholsome | "Chicasaw Plumb" | 1 |
| 53 | *Glycine frutescens* [*Wisteria frutescens*] | A rambling florobundant climber; the blossoms in large pendant clusters, of a fine celestial blue, well adapted for covering arbors | "Kidney Bean Tree," wisteria | 3 |
| 54 | *Æsculus pavia* | | Red buckeye | |

*Charles Willson Peale,*
William Bartram, *1808.*

| No. | Plant | Description | Common name(s) | Number of plants |
|---|---|---|---|---|
| 55 | Æ[sculus] varietas | their light & airy foliage, crimson & variegated flowers, present a gay & mirthful appearance; continually, whilst in bloom visited by the brilliant thundering Humingbird. The root of this Tree is esteemed preferable to soap, for scouring & cleansing woolen Cloths. | | 2 |
| 56 | Æsculus virginica | beautiful foliage Flowers pale yellow | Yellow horse chestnut | 1 |
| 57 | Æsculus alba | The branches terminate with long erect spikes of sweet white flowers | | 1 |
| 58 | Juniperus sabina | Evergreen | Savin | 1 |
| 59 | Evonimus americanus [Euonymus americanus] | evergreen, presents a fine appearance in Autumn, with crimson fruit | spindle tree | 1 |
| 60 | Prunus Laurus cerasus [Prunus laurocerasus] | A beautiful evergreen tree of Europe; its green leaves are said to possess a dangerous deleterious quality | cherry laurel, English laurel | 1 |
| 61 | Yucca filamentosa | beautiful ornamental evergreen | Adam's needle | 2 |
| 62 | Yucca gloriosa | flowering plants | Spanish dagger | |
| 63 | Myrica gale | possesses an highly aromatic, and very agreeable scent | "Bog gale," sweet gale, bog myrtle | 4 |
| 64 | Platanus orientalis | a famous tree celebrated for the beauty of his foliage, expansion, and grateful shade he affords | Oriental sycamore, oriental plane | 2 |
| 65 | Amorpha fruticosa | | Bastard indigo | 1 |
| 66 | Amorpha caerulia [caerulea] | Foliage light and delicately pennated, garnished with flowers of a fine | Bastard indigo | 2 |
| 67 | Salix variegata | Silver blotched willow | | 1 |
| 68 | Mespilus nivea | An early flowering shrub, of uncommon elegance | (Snowy mespilus), Medlar | 1 |
| 69 | Mesp[ilus]. pubescens | Somewhat resembling the foregoing; but of less stature & the flowers not so large, nor of so clean a white: both produce very pleasant fruit | | 2 |
| 70 | Mesp[ilus]. pusilla | flowers early, the blossoms white & abundant; exhibits a fine appearance | | 1 |

| No. | Plant | Description | Common name(s) | Number of plants |
|-----|-------|-------------|----------------|------------------|
| 71 | Mesp[ilus]. prunifolia [Aronia prunifolia] | Presents a good appearance, when all red with its clusters of berries | chokeberry | 1 |
| 72 | Colutia [Colutea] arborescens | exhibits a good appearance, foliage pinnated, of a soft pleasant green, colour, interspersed with the large yellow papillionacious flowers, in succession | Bladder senna | 3 |
| 73 | Rhus Italicum | | Sumac | 1 |
| 74 | Mespilus pyracantha [Pyracantha coccinea] | a beautiful flower[in]g shrub, evergreen in mild seasons | firethorn | 4 |
| 75 | Itea virginiana [or virginica] | a handsome flower[in]g shrub | Virginia sweetspire, Virginia willow, tassel-white | 3 |
| 76 | Cornus alba | white berried swamp Dogwood | | 1 |
| 77 | Prunus divaricata [Prunus cerasifera divaricata] | diciduous, flowers white in raumes [racemes], stems diverging & branches pendulous | cherry plum | 2 |
| 78 | Hydrangia [Hydrangea] arborescens | Ornamental in shruberies, flowers white in large corymbes | | 3 |
| 79 | Andromeda axil[l]aris | Evergreen | Bog rosemary | 1 |
| 80 | Acer pumilum | handsome shrub for coppices, foliage singular, younger shoots red | Dwarf maple | 3 |
| 81 | Amygdalus persica, flore pleno [Prunus persica, flore pleno] | of great splendour & amiable presence | double-flowered peach | 1 |
| 82 | Magnolia glauca [Magnolia virginiana] | charming—the milk-white roseate blossom possesses an animating fragrance | "Rose Laurel," sweet bay, swamp magnolia | 1 |
| 83 | Sambucus rubra [Sambucus canadensis] | early flowering and handsome; its coral red berries in large clusters, ripe abt midsummer | American elder, sweet elder | 1 |
| 84 | Rubus odoratus | foliage beautiful; flowers of the figure, colour & fragrance of the rose | Flowering raspberry, thimbleberry | 3 |
| 85 | Rosa Pennsylvanica flor: pleno [Rosa palustris] | flowers monthly from May 'till Novembr | swamp rose | 2 |
| 86 | Lonicera inodora | Twine's round, & ascends trees spreading its bloom over their boughs | Honeysuckle | 1 |

| No. | Plant | Description | Common name(s) | Number of plants |
|---|---|---|---|---|
| 87 | *Ribes oxyacanthoides [Grossularia canadenis]* | fruit small & smooth | "Prickly Gooseberry" | 1 |
| 88 | *Populus balsamifera* | foliage beautiful, its buds in the spring replete with an odoriferous balsam | Balsam poplar | 1 |
| 89 | *Crategus [Crataegus] aria* | foliage beautiful; silvered with white cottony down, underside | Hawthorn | 1 |
| 90 | *Pt[e]lea trifoliata* | singular | (call'd the foil tree), "Trefoil Tree," hop tree | 2 |
| 91 | *Lonicera symphoricarpos* | singular; appears well in winter when garnished with clusters of red berries | "Indian Currants" | 1 |
| 92 | *Laurus nobilis* | Sweet Bay, a celebrated Evergreen—leaves odoriferous | "Red Bay," bay laurel, sweet bay | 1 |
| 93 | *Rhus triphyllum* | Singular early flowering shrub | "Poison Oak," sumac | 5 |
| 94 | *Citisus laburnum [Cytisus laburnum, Laburnum anagyroides]* | foliage delicate, embellished with pendant clusters of splendid yellow papillionacious flowers | golden-chain | 1 |
| 95 | *Periploca graeca* | climbing up trees & shrubs; flowers very singular | Silk vine | 2 |
| 96 | *Hibiscus coccineus* | a most elegant flowering plant; flowers large, of a splendid crimson colour | Scarlet rosemallow | 1 |
| 97 | *Bignonia crucigera* | A climber, mounting to the tops of trees & buildings; flowers abundant | "Cross Vine," trumpet flower | 1 |
| 98 | *Bignonia semper virens* | A climber as famous, at least for the richness of his robe; flowers of a splendid golden yellow, & odoriferous; very proper for covering arbors &c. | "Yellow Jasmin" | 2 |
| 99 | *Betula (alnus) maritima [Alnus maritima, betula]* | singular; retains his verdure very late in the autumn | "Sea side Alder" | 2 |
| 100 | *Amygdalus pumila, flor: pleno [Prunus pumila, flore pleno]* | A most elegant flowering shrub; ornimental in vases for Court yards &c. | sand or dwarf cherry, dwarf doubleflowering almond | 1 |
| 101 | *Arundo donax* | Maiden Cane | | 1 |

| No. | Plant | Description | Common name(s) | Number of plants |
|-----|-------|-------------|----------------|------------------|
| 102 | *Callicarpa americana* | Very shewy & pleasing; the flowers of a delicate incarnate hue, & vast clusters of purple berries | "Bermudas Mulberry," French mulberry, American beautyberry | 1 |
| 103 | *Syringa persica* | elegant; its flexile stems terminate with heavy panicles of purple blossoms, of animating fragrance | (Persian Lilac) | 2 |
| 104 | *Mimosa virgata* | Singularly beautiful in its plumed foliage— native of Pearl Island near the Misisipi | | 1 |
| 105 | *Punica granatum flor. plen:* | the figure & splendour of its flowers exceed description | Pomegranate | 1 |
| 106 | *Aristolochia sipho.* [*Aristolochia macrophylla*] | Climbs & spreads over trees & other supports, to a great height & distance: flowers of singular figure; its abundant large leaves, present it as a vine well adapted for covering arbors | Dutchman's pipe | 1 |

# Plants from John Bartram's Nursery, November 1792

When George Washington's initial delivery of plants from the Bartram nursery arrived at Mount Vernon, in the spring of 1792, farm manager George Augustine Washington reported that they had been allowed to grow for too long in their shipping boxes and, as a result, "came out in a very tender state."[5] The gardener, John Christian Ehlers, was unable to graft the plants in their delicate condition, and he doubted they would survive. Indeed, many of them died during the summer, and in November the president sent replacement plants; these were accompanied by a list drawn up by Washington's secretary Bartholomew Dandridge, Jr., who was a nephew of Martha Washington.[6]

At the bottom of the list, George Washington added specific instructions, in his own hand, for the placement of these plants in oval beds on either side of the bowling green, correcting the work that George Augustine Washington and Ehlers had done in the spring. The president included the heights of the trees on this list so that his gardeners could determine the appropriate location for each one within the ovals. He wanted the largest trees planted in the center of the ovals and the shrubs placed in descending heights, from the center out to the edges. Departing from his symmetrical approach to planting the bowling green itself, he directed that "except the large trees for the Centre & sides no regularity may be observed in planting the others in the Ovals."[7]

| No. | Plant | Description | Common name(s) | Number of plants |
|---|---|---|---|---|
| 2 | Ulex europeus | embellished with sweet scented flowers of a fine yellow colour | Furze | |
| 3 | Hypericum kalmianum | profusely garnished with fine gold coloured blossoms | "Shrub St. John's wort" | 2 |
| 4 | Hyperi: Angustifolium | Evergreen, adorned with fine yellow flowers | | |
| 5 | Taxus procumbens | Evergreen, of a splendid full green throughout the year—red berries | Yew | |
| 6 | Buxus aureis [aureus] | Elegant, called gilded box | | |
| 7 | Daphne mezerium [mezereum] | an early flowering sweet scented little shrub | Mezereon, paradise plant | |
| 8 | Calycanthus floridus | Odoriferous, it's blossoms scented like the Pine Apple | "Sweet Shrub of Carolina," Carolina allspice | |
| 10 | Æsculus hippocastanum | a magnificent flowering and shady tree | Horse chestnut | |

List of Trees Shrubs &c had of Jnº Bartram to supply
the place of those of his Catalogue of Mar: 92. which failed.

Novʳ 7ᵗʰ 1792.
Soot hist.

Nº 2. d Ulex europeus E. grows from 3 to 4. embellished with sweet scented
flowers of a fine yellow colour.

2. 3. Hypericum kalmianum    3 to 4. profusely garnished with fine
gold coloured blossoms — 2 plants.

4. Hyperic.    Angustifolium  3 to 6. Evergreen, adorned with fine
yellow flowers.

c. 5. Taxus procumbens      3 to 6. Evergreen — of a splendid dull
green throughout the year — red berries.

6. Buxus aureus E.      3 to 10. Elegant, called gilded box.

7. Daphne mezerium E.    1 to 3. an early flowering sweet scented
little shrub.

8. Calycanthus floridus    4 to 8. odoriferous. its blossoms scented
like the Pine apple.

E. 10. Æsculus hippocastanum. 20, 40 to 50. a magnificent flowering
and shady tree.

11. Evonimus atrapurpurius. — 6 to 8. its fruit of a bright crimson in
the autumn (burning bush) 3 plants.

13. Franklinia.        3, 15 to 20. flowers large, white and
fragrant. Native of Georgia.

16. Kalmia angustifolia    1 to 2. Evergreen garnished with
crimson speckled flowers. 4 plants.

24. Halesia tetraptera    4, 10 to 15. flowers abundant, white, of
the shape of little bells.

25. Viburnum opulifolium  3 to 7. of singular beauty in flower & fruit

27. Viburnum alnifolium .  3 to 6 handsome flowering shrub.

29. Sorbus sativa E.      10, 15. 30. its fruit pear & apple shaped,
as large & well tasted when mellow.

31. Sorbus aucuparia    8. 15 to 30 of foliage elegant: embellished
with umbels of coral red berries.

c. 36. Stewartia malachodendron 5 to 8. floriferous. the flowers large
and white, embellished with a large tuft of black or purple thread in their centre.

38. Styrax grandifolium.  3 to 10. a most charming flowering shrub
blossoms snow white, & of the most grateful scent. (called snow-drop tree.)

39. Philadelphus coronarius E. 4. 10. a sweet flowering shrub. (called
mock orange).

40. Philadelphus inodorus  5. 7. 10. his robe a silver flowered mantle.

c. 41. Pinus strobus      50. 80. 100. magnificent! he presides in the
evergreen groves (White Pine). 4 plants.
carr.ᵈ over

357-33

*First page of "List of Trees, Shrubs &c had of Jno. Bartram*
*to supply the place of those of his Catalogue of Mar: 92.*
*Which failed," November 1792.*

| No. | Plant | Description | Common name(s) | Number of plants |
|---|---|---|---|---|
| 11 | Euonimus atrapurpurius [Euonymus atropurpureus] | It's fruit of a bright crimson in the autumn | (burning bush) | 3 |
| 13 | Franklinia [alatamaha] | flowers large, white and fragrant. Native of Georgia | Franklin tree | |
| 16 | Kalmia angustifolia | Evergreen. garnished with crimson speckled flowers | "Thyme leav'd Kalmia," lambkill, sheep laurel | 4 |
| 24 | Halesia tetraptera [or carolina] | flowers abundant, white, of the shape of little bells | Carolina silverbell | |
| 25 | Viburnum opulifolium | of singular beauty in flower & fruit | | |
| 27 | Viburnum alnifolium [Viburnum lantanoides] | handsome flowering shrub | hobble bush | |
| 29 | Sorbus Sativa [prob. Sorbus domestica] | It's fruit pear & apple shaped, as large & well tasted when mellow | prob. service tree | |
| 31 | Sorbus aucuparia | foliage elegant: embellished with umbells of coral red berries | European mountain ash | |
| 36 | Stewartia malachodendron | floriferous. the flowers large and white, embellished with a large tuft of black or purple threads in their centre | Silky stewartia or stuartia | |
| 38 | Styrax grandifolium | a most charming flowering shrub, blossoms snow white, & of the most grateful scent | (call'd Snow-drop tree), Snowbell, storax | |
| 39 | Philadelphus coronarius | a sweet flowering shrub | (called mock Orange) | |
| 40 | Philadelphus inodorus | his robe a silver flowered mantle | | |
| 41 | Pinus Strobus | magnificent! he presides in the ever green Groves | (white pine) | 4 |
| 42 | Pinus communis | a stately tree, foliage of a Seagreen colour; and exhibits a good appearance whilst young | (Scotch Fir) | |
| 43 | Pinus Larix | Elegant figure & foliage | "Larch Tree" | |
| 45 | Robinia villosa | a gay shrub enrobed with plum'd leaves & roseat flowers | "Peach Blossom Acacia" | 3 |

| No. | Plant | Description | Common name(s) | Number of plants |
|---|---|---|---|---|
| 52 | *Prunus chicasa* | Early flowering, very fruitful; the fruit nearly round, cleft, red, purple, yellow, of an inticing look, most agreeable taste & wholesome | (chicasaw Plumb) | |
| 57 | *Æsculus alba* | The branches terminate with long erect spikes of sweet white flowers | | |
| 58 | *Juniperus sabina* | Evergreen | Savin | |
| 54 | *Æsculus pavia* | It's light and airy foliage crimson & variegated flowers, present a gay and mirthful appearance; continually, whilst in bloom, visited by the brilliant thundering Humingbird. The root of the tree is esteemed preferable to Soap, for scouring & cleaning woolen clothes. | Red buckeye | 2 |
| 63 | *Myrica gale* | possesses an highly aromatic, and very agreeable scent | "Bog gale," sweet gale, bog myrtle | 3 |
| 69 | *Mespilus pubescens* | an early flowering shrub of great elegance, produces very pleasant fruit | | 2 |
| 72 | *Colutia [Colutea] arborescens* | Exhibits a good appearance; foliage pinnated, of a soft pleasant green colour, interspers'd with large yellow papillionacious flowers in succession | Bladder senna | |
| 77 | *Prunus Divaricata [Prunus cerasifera divaricata]* | deciduous, flowers white in raumes [racemes], stems diverging & branches pendulous | cherry plum | |
| 78 | *Hydrangia [Hydrangea] arborescens* | Ornamental in shruberies, flowers white in large corymbes | | |
| 79 | *Andromeda exilaris [axillaris]* | Evergreen | Bog rosemary | |
| 80 | *Acer pumilum; s, montanum* | handsome shrub for coppices. foliage singular, younger shoots, red | Dwarf maple | |
| 84 | *Rubus odoratus* | foliage beautiful; flowers of the figure, colour & fragrance of the rose | Flowering raspberry, thimbleberry | |
| 92 | *Laurus nobilis* | Sweet Bay; a celebrated evergreen—leaves odoriferous | "Red Bay," bay laurel, sweet bay | |

| No. | Plant | Description | Common name(s) | Number of plants |
|---|---|---|---|---|
| 101 | *Arundo donax* | Maiden Cane | | |
| | *In addition to the above,* | | | |
| 1 | *Mespilus pyracantha* [Pyracantha coccinea] | Evergreen Thorn. a very beautiful flowering shrub; in flower & fruit. evergreen in moderate climates, and not to be exceeded in usefulness, for hedges Fences &ca. | firethorn | |

# Upper Garden Plants

The following plants are documented as appearing in the upper garden, either in George Washington's writings or in visitors' accounts. Visitors who noted specific plants were Benjamin Henry Latrobe (July 19, 1796), Amariah Frost (June 26, 1797), Julian Ursyn Niemcewicz (June 2, 1798), and the Reverend John E. Latta (July 3, 1799).[8]

## FRUITS AND NUTS

Apples
  *Gloucester White apples*
  *Maryland Red Strick apples*
  *New Town Pippins*
  *Young crab apples*
Apricots
Cherries
  *Black May Heart cherries*
  *Bullock Heart cherries*
  *Coronation cherries*
  *Duke cherries*
  *Early May cherries*
  *May Duke cherries*
  *May White Heart cherries*
Currants ‡
Fig trees ‡
Gooseberries ‡
Grapes
  *English grapes* ‡
  *Madeira grapes*
Kentucky coffee tree *
Lemon trees
Limes ‡
Mississippi nuts
Mulberries
  *English mulberries* ‡
  *Mulberry cuttings*

Orange Burgamots
Orange trees
Paliuris (Christ's thorn)
Palmetto royal
Peaches
Pears
  *Burgamy pears*
  *Bury pears*
  *Butter pears*
  *Early June pears*
  *Pear of Worcester*
  *St. Germain pears*
  *Spanish pears*
  *Summer Boon Chrns.*
    *[bon chrétien] pears*
  *Winter Boon Chrns.*
    *[bon chrétien] pears*
Pistachio nut *
Plums
  *Cherokee plums*
  *Magnum Bonum plums*
Quinces
Raisins ‡
Raspberries ‡
Scarlet Alpine strawberry seeds ‡
Sower orange *
Strawberries ‡

Walnuts
  *English walnuts*
  *French walnuts*

## VEGETABLES

Artichokes ‡
Beans
Beets
Broccoli
Cabbage
Carrots
Cauliflower
Celery
Early corn
Kidney beans
Leeks
Lettuce
Onions
Peas
Radishes

## EXOTICS AND ORNAMENTALS

Aloe
Balm-scented shrub
Boxwood ‡
Catalpa
French honeysuckle
Honey locust
Horse chestnut *
Lilies ‡
Live oak *
Magnolia or laurel of Carolina *
Magnolia *
Mahogany *
Pinks ‡
Poppies ‡
Rhamnus trees (buckthorn)
Roses ‡
Seedgrass
Shaddocks (lime, lemon)
"Simlens"

‡ Plants mentioned only in visitors' accounts, prior to December 1799 (and not in Washington's own correspondence or diaries).

* Plants placed in boxes in front of the greenhouse, rather than in the garden beds.

# Trees, Shrubs, and Vines

The following trees, shrubs, and vines are mentioned in George Washington's correspondence and diaries. They were variously dug from forests on his eight-thousand-acre property, sent to him at his request, or received by Washington as gifts. All were planted on the Mount Vernon grounds.[9]

### TREES

Acacia, acasse (*Albizia julibrissin*)

Althea tree (*Hibiscus syriacus*)

Ash (*Fraxinus americana*)

Aspen (*Populus tremuloides*)

Blackgum (*Nyssa sylvatica*)

Blackhaw (*Viburnum prunifolium*)

Buckeye (*Aesculus pavia*)

Catalpa (*Catalpa bignonioides*)

Chestnut, common (*Castanea dentata*)

Cobb nuts (*Coryulus avellana*)

Crapemyrtle (*Lagerstroemia indica*)

Cypress, pyramidal (*Cupressus sempervirens*)

Dogwood (*Cornus florida*)

Elm (*Ulmus americana*)

Filbert (*Corylus maxima*)

Fringe tree (*Chionanthus virginica*)

Hemlock (*Tsuga Canadensis*)

Hickory (*Carya ovata*)

Hickory, shellbark (*Carya laciniosa*)

Holly (*Ilex opaca*)

Honey locust (*Gleditsia triacanthos*)

Kentucky coffee tree (*Gymnocladus dioicus*)

Linden (*Tilia americana*)

Live oak (*Quercus virginiana*)

Locust (*Robinia pseudoacacia*)

Magnolia (*Magnolia grandiflora*)

Magnolia, swamp (*Magnolia virginiana*)

Mahogany (*Swietenia mahogani*)

Maple (*Acer rubrum*)

Mulberry, black (*Morus nigra*)

Mulberry, red (*Morus rubra*)

Mulberry, white (*Morus alba*)

Oak, burr (*Quercus macrocarpa*)

Oak, water (*Quercus nigra*)

Palmetto, royal (*Sabal unbraculifera*)

Pawpaw (*Asiminia triloba*)

Pecan (*Carya illinoinensis*)

Pistachio (*Pistatia*)

Pine (*Pinus virginiana*)

Pine, Mediterranean (*Pinus pinea*)

Poplar, Lombardy (*Populus nigra italica*)

Poplar, tulip (*Liriodendron tulipifera*)

Pride of China (*Melia azedarach*)

Redbud (*Cercis canadensis*)

Rhamnus (*Rhamnus alaternus*)

Sandbox tree (*Hura crepitans*)

Sassafras (*Sassafras albidum*)

Spruce (*Picea glauca*)

Sycamore (*Platanus occidentalis*)

Thorn, large-berried (*Crataegus punctata*)

Thorn, small-berried (*Crataegus spathulata*)

Willow, weeping (*Salix babylonica*)

### SHRUBS

Boxwood, edging
(*Buxus sempervirens suffruticosa*)

Boxwood, tree
(*Buxus sempervirens arborescens*)

Guelder rose (*Viburnum opulus*)

Honeysuckle, wood
(*Rhododendron nudiflorum*)

Hydrangea (*Hydrangea quercifolia*)

Ivy (*Kalmia latifolia*)

Jessamine, Persian (*Syringa persica*)

Laurel (*Kalmia latifolia*)

Lilac (*Syringa vulgaris*)

Swamp red-berry bush (*Ilex verticillata*)

Sweetbriar (*Rosa eglanteria*)

Willow, yellow (*Salix alba vitellina*)

Yew (*Taxus baccata*)

### VINES

Honeysuckle, scarlet
(*Lonicera sempervirens*)

Honeysuckle, woodbine
(*Lonicera periclymenum*)

Jessamine, yellow
(*Gelseminum sempervirens*)

PRECEDING SPREAD: *View toward Mansion from serpentine path along north edge of bowling green, 2014.* ABOVE: *Espaliered apple tree in lower garden, 2012.*

# About the Contributors

ADAM T. ERBY, Assistant Curator at Mount Vernon, was lead curator of the exhibition *Gardens & Groves: George Washington's Landscape at Mount Vernon* (2014–16). He is currently at work on several room-restoration projects and interpretive scenarios. Erby holds a BA in American studies from the University of Virginia and an MA from the University of Delaware's Winterthur Program in American Material Culture. The main focus of his research is on the arts and cultures of the American South during the eighteenth and nineteenth centuries, with an emphasis on plantation architecture and interiors. He co-authored the article "'The one Mrs. Trist would chuse': Thomas Jefferson, the Trist Family, and the Monticello Campeachy" for the 2012 edition of *American Furniture*.

J. DEAN NORTON, Director of Horticulture, began working at Mount Vernon at age sixteen. In 1977, having earned a BS in ornamental horticulture from Clemson University, he took up full-time duties at the estate. The main focus of his research is on eighteenth-century gardens and gardening practices. He has lectured both nationally and abroad and is the recipient of numerous conservation honors, including the American Horticultural Society's Professional Award in 2006. Norton serves on the boards of several historic sites, is a past president of the Southern Garden History Society, and was named an honorary member of the Garden Club of Virginia in 2010.

SUSAN P. SCHOELWER is Robert H. Smith Senior Curator at Mount Vernon, where she has directed the refurnishing and reinterpretation of George Washington's "New Room," the reinstallation of the greenhouse slave quarter, and other exhibition and furnishing projects. She holds a PhD in American studies from Yale University, an MA from the University of Delaware's Winterthur Program in Early American Culture, and a BA in history from the University of Notre Dame. Schoelwer was previously head of museum collections at the Connecticut Historical Society, Hartford, and taught at Virginia Commonwealth, Villanova, and Rutgers universities. She has edited books on Connecticut Valley furniture, early American tavern signs, western American art, and the Alamo, and she has written and lectured on American decorative and fine arts, material culture, and Mount Vernon.

ESTHER C. WHITE, Director of Historic Preservation, heads Mount Vernon's ongoing program devoted to the long-term care and researching of George Washington's home. For nearly two decades before assuming her present position, in 2012, White directed the estate's archaeology program—designed to research, preserve, and interpret Mount Vernon's buried resources; she led excavations at the upper garden, Washington's distillery, and the south grove midden. She earned a BA in history at the University of North Carolina, Chapel Hill; an MA in anthropology, with specialization in historical archaeology, at the College of William and Mary, Williamsburg, Virginia; and a PhD in archaeology from the University of Leicester, England. White is the coauthor, with Dennis J. Pogue, of *George Washington's Gristmill at Mount Vernon* (2005).

ANDREA WULF was born in India, reared in Germany, and lives in England. Her book *The Brother Gardeners: Botany, Empire, and the Birth of an Obsession* (2008) won the American Horticultural Society's book award in 2010. Wulf's *Founding Gardeners: The Revolutionary Generation, Nature, and the Shaping of the American Nation* (2011) was a *New York Times* best seller. She was the Eccles British Library Writer in Residence in 2013 and is a three-time fellow of the International Center for Jefferson Studies at Monticello. She has written for the *New York Times*, *Guardian*, and *Los Angeles Times*, is a regular contributor to BBC radio and TV programs, and has lectured widely in the United Kingdom and the United States.

# Chapter Notes

## FREQUENTLY CITED SOURCES AND ABBREVIATIONS

GW
George Washington

GWD
Donald Jackson and Dorothy Twohig, eds. *The Diaries of George Washington*. 6 vols. (Charlottesville: University Press of Virginia, 1976–79)

MVLA
Mount Vernon Ladies' Association of the Union

MVLA AR
Mount Vernon Ladies' Association of the Union Annual Report

PGW Digital
Theodore J. Crackel, Edward G. Lengel et al., eds. *The Papers of George Washington, Digital Edition* (Charlottesville: University of Virginia Press, Rotunda, 2008).

Smith Library, Mount Vernon
The Fred W. Smith National Library for the Study of George Washington at Mount Vernon

## FOREWORD

1. GW to Lund Washington, Aug. 19, 1776, PGW Digital.
2. Tobias Lear, The Last Illness and Death of General Washington, December 14, 1799, PGW Digital.

## DESIGNING THE BEAUTIFUL: *General Washington's Landscape Improvements, 1784–1787*

1. Julian Ursyn Niemcewicz, *Under Their Vine and Fig Tree: Travels through America in 1797–1799, 1805, with Some Further Account of Life in New Jersey*, trans. and ed. Metchie J. E. Budka (Elizabeth, N.J.: Grassmann Publishing, 1965), 98.
2. Two recently published books consider George Washington as a landscape designer: Joseph Manca, *George Washington's Eye: Landscape, Architecture, and Design at Mount Vernon* (Baltimore: Johns Hopkins University Press, 2012); and Andrea Wulf, *Founding Gardeners: The Revolutionary Generation, Nature, and the Shaping of the American Nation* (New York: Alfred A. Knopf, 2011). For an extensive discussion of the evolution of landscape design in America, see Ann Leighton, *American Gardens in the Eighteenth Century: "For Use or for Delight"* (Amherst: University of Massachusetts Press, 1986).
3. For the early history of Mount Vernon, see Robert F. Dalzell, Jr., and Lee Baldwin Dalzell, *George Washington's Mount Vernon: At Home in Revolutionary America* (New York: Oxford University Press, 1998), 47–73. Washington acquired full title to Mount Vernon in 1762, after the death of his sister-in-law Ann Fairfax Washington Lee.
4. GW to Robert Cary & Company, Invoice, May 1, 1759, PGW Digital.
5. Batty Langley, *New Principles of Gardening; or, The Laying out and Planting of Parterres, Groves, Wildernesses, Labyrinths, Avenues, Parks, &c.* (London: Printed for A. Bettesworth and J. Batley, 1728).
6. Ibid., iii–x; Charles Quest-Ritson, *The English Garden: A Social History* (Boston: David R. Godine, 2001), 122–29.
7. For more on picturesque landscapes, see John Dixon Hunt, *The Picturesque Garden in Europe* (London: Thames and Hudson, 2002).

8. GW to Richard Washington, Invoice, Apr. 25, 1757, PGW Digital.

9. For portraits of the Virginia gentry, see Carolyn J. Weekley, *Painters and Paintings of the Early American South* (New Haven and London: Yale University Press, 2013). Charles Willson Peale's portraits of George Washington are illustrated and discussed on pp. 357–63.

10. For George Washington as an art collector, see "Washington as Gardener: Creating the Landscape," in Manca, *George Washington's Eye*, 83–119.

11. Dalzell and Dalzell, *George Washington's Mount Vernon*, 100–28.

12. GW to Lund Washington, Aug. 19, 1776, PGW Digital. The British attack began on the night of August 21, 1776, two days after Washington penned this letter.

13. GW to Arthur Young, Dec. 12, 1793, PGW Digital.

14. The north "necessary" had been removed by 1787 when Samuel Vaughan recorded the landscape, but the south one was not removed until 1796. See GW to William Pearce, May 29, 1796, PGW Digital.

15. Benson J. Lossing, *Mount Vernon and Its Associations: Historical, Biographical, and Pictorial* (New York: W. A. Townsend, 1859), 154–55. Mount Vernon scholars have debated whether the map Lossing saw was George Washington's original plan, because the letters on the map do not exactly correspond with a lettered list of trees in Washington's hand. I contend that Lossing was looking to give the overall effect of the map rather than create a precise reproduction. As in most of his drawings, he took artistic liberties and did not replicate the letters exactly as he saw them. He may simply have noted that there were letters in these locations and filled them in later.

16. The location of the original tree list is not known; an illustration of it appears in Benson J. Lossing, "Mount Vernon as It Is," *Harper's New Monthly Magazine* 18, no. 106 (Mar. 1859): 443. Lossing's copy of George Washington's memorandum on trees appears only in his *Harper's* article and not in his book on Mount Vernon. In the *Harper's* article, Lossing recorded buildings and objects he saw at the estate during the years John Augustine Washington III owned it (1842–60), and it seems likely that the two drawings and the memorandum were in Washington's possession at that time. The letters on the general plan and section do not correspond exactly with the memorandum in Washington's hand; there are two possible reasons for this. The first is that Lossing may have sketched just enough details of the plan to give the effect of the design and then filled in the details, including the letters, later. This is often the case when Lossing's drawings are compared with the objects they are intended to represent. The other possibility is that Washington revised his design as he worked through the details and that these documents reflect two different stages in that process.

17. GW to William Pearce, Dec. 23, 1793, PGW Digital. For the divisions between the white and black areas of Virginia plantations, see Dell Upton, "White and Black Landscapes in Eighteenth-Century Virginia," *Places* 2, no. 2 (1984): 59–72.

18. See Mac Griswold, *Washington's Gardens at Mount Vernon: Landscape of the Inner Man* (Boston: Houghton Mifflin, 1999); and Elizabeth Kellam de Forest, *The Gardens and Grounds at Mount Vernon: How George Washington Planned and Planted Them* (Mount Vernon: MVLA, 1982).

19. Philip Miller, *The Abridgement of the Gardener's Dictionary* (London: For the author, 1763). For the use of gardening literature in the eighteenth century, see Therese O'Malley, "Appropriation and Adaptation: Early Gardening Literature in America," *Huntington Library Quarterly* 55, no. 3 (Summer 1992): 401–33.

20. Entry for June 10, 1787, GWD, 5: 166–67.

21. Although Washington's visit to Mount Clare is not recorded in his diaries, it is likely that he either visited or heard of the home when he was in Annapolis in December 1783 to resign his military commission. For his interest in Mrs. Carroll's greenhouse, see GW to Tench Tilghman, Aug. 11, 1784, and Tench Tilghman to GW, Aug. 18 1784, PGW Digital.

22. Entry for Mar. 13, 1748, GWD, 1: 7.

23. Entry for Jan. 12, 1785, GWD, 4: 76–77.

24. Ibid.

25. Entry for Jan. 19, 1785, GWD, 4: 78–79. For more on Washington's work laying out the landscape in the winter and early spring of 1785, see his diary entries between Jan. 20 and Mar. 31, GWD, 4: 78–120

26. GW to George Augustine Washington, Jan. 6, 1785, PGW Digital.

27. GW to George Clinton, Apr. 20, 1785, PGW Digital.

28. Entry for Mar. 8–9, 1785, GWD, 4: 86–87.

29. Entry for Apr. 16, 1785, GWD, 4: 121–22.

30. Ibid. By the time Samuel Vaughan arrived at Mount Vernon, in August 1787, the plantings had taken root and were beginning to grow.

31. GW to John Washington, Mar. 20, 1773, PGW Digital.

32. Entry for Nov. 14, 1788, GWD, 5: 422.
33. Tobias Lear to Clement Biddle, Sept. 16, 1789, PGW Digital; John Christian Ehlers to GW, June 24, 1789, PGW Digital.
34. M. Kent Brinkley, "The Professional Gardener's Trade in the Eighteenth Century," *Magnolia* 13, no. 3 (Fall 1997): 1–10.
35. Mary V. Thompson, "Slaves on the Mansion House Farm," unpublished research report, 2013, MVLA.
36. GW to Anthony Whitting, Oct. 14, 1792, PGW Digital. Washington retained many of the weekly reports from both his gardener and his farm manger; these are accessible via PGW Digital.
37. For Washington's decision not to retain Ehlers when the gardener's contract expired, see GW to James Anderson, Apr. 7, 1797, PGW Digital. For his earlier admonition to Ehlers to curtail his use of alcohol, see GW to John Christian Ehlers, Dec. 23, 1793, PGW Digital.
38. GW to James Anderson, Apr. 7, 1797; Anderson to GW, Aug. 3 and Nov. 4, 1797, PGW Digital.
39. GW to James Anderson, July 25, 1798, PGW Digital.
40. Sarah P. Stetson, "The Philadelphia Sojourn of Samuel Vaughan," *Pennsylvania Magazine of History and Biography* 73, no. 4 (Oct. 1949): 459–74. For the mantel, see Carol Borchert Cadou, *The George Washington Collection: Fine and Decorative Arts at Mount Vernon* (Manchester, Vt.: Hudson Hills Press, 2006), 102–4.
41. GW to Samuel Vaughan, Nov. 12, 1787, PGW Digital. For more on Vaughan's presentation drawing, see Manca, *George Washington's Eye*, 88–89, 102–4.
42. GW to Joseph Rakestraw, July 20, 1787, PGW Digital.
43. For the Mount Vernon weathervane, see Cadou, *George Washington Collection*, 122–23.

## George Washington's Gardens:
### Under the Watchful Eye of the Mount Vernon Ladies

The chapter-opening quotation is from Ann Pamela Cunningham's farewell address to the Vice Regents at the Council of 1874, upon her retirement as regent. MVLA Minutes, 1874, 5. The address is now reprinted in the MVLA Minutes every year.

1. John A. Harper to Eliza Jane [daughter], Nov. 29, 1812, manuscript collection, Smith Library, Mount Vernon.
2. William Mercer Green diary, 1818, excerpt transcribed in Early Descriptions of Mount Vernon, 1800–1841, vol. 1, Black Notebook Collection, no. 16, Smith Library, Mount Vernon.
3. Raconteur, "On the Potomac: Correspondence of the [New-York] *Commercial Advertiser*," *States and Union* (Washington, D.C.), July 19, 1860, RM-306/NEWS-2960, Smith Library, Mount Vernon; transcribed in Early Descriptions of Mount Vernon, 1842–, Black Notebook Collection, no. 18, Smith Library, Mount Vernon.
4. "Visit to Mount Vernon, from the Woonsocket Patriot," *Herald*, Nov. 1844, transcribed in Early Descriptions of Mount Vernon, 1842–, Black Notebook Collection, no. 18, Smith Library, Mount Vernon.
5. "Copy of Memoir dictated by Fannie Keith Arnold about her aunt Sara Tracy (Herbert)," n.d., typescript, information files, Smith Library, Mount Vernon.
6. Report of Green-house Committee, MVLA Minutes, 1883, 19. For Whelan's arrival, see MVLA Minutes, 1881, 16.
7. Report of the Committee on Garden and Green-houses, MVLA Minutes, 1911, 66.
8. GW, "A Journal of my Journey over the Mountains," entry for Mar. 13, 1748, PGW Digital.
9. Entry for Jan. 12, 1785, GWD, 4: 75.
10. MVLA AR 1870, 4.
11. Report of Superintendent: Trimming Trees, MVLA Minutes, 1902, 47.
12. [Report of the Regent,] MVLA Minutes, 1915, 16.
13. Charles Sprague Sargent, *The Trees at Mount Vernon* (repr. from MVLA Minutes, 1917), 62. For more on Sargent, see S. B. Sutton, *Charles Sprague Sargent and the Arnold Arboretum* (Cambridge, Mass.: Harvard University Press, 1970).
14. Charles Sprague Sargent, *The Trees at Mount Vernon*, rev. ed. (repr. from MVLA AR, 1926).
15. Report of Landscape Architect, MVLA Minutes, 1933, 42–43. For the initial contact with Williams and Abbott, see Annual Report of the Regent, MVLA Minutes, 1932, 12–13.
16. Report of the Kitchen Garden Committee, MVLA Minutes, 1936, 44–45.
17. Report of the Committee on Special Publications, MVLA Minutes, 1938, 68.
18. Report of the Kitchen Garden Committee, MVLA Minutes, 1936, 45.
19. Robert B. Fisher and Charles Cecil Wall, "A List of Ornamental Trees and Shrubs Noted in the Writings of George Washington," unpublished report, circa 1950, Smith Library, Mount Vernon.

20. [Hetty Cary Harrison,] *The Mount Vernon Gardens, with Notes Pertaining to the Domestic Life of George and Martha Washington* (Mount Vernon: MVLA [circa 1941]; Robert B. Fisher, *The Mount Vernon Gardens: A Brief Description of Their Origin and Restoration, Complete Plant Lists, Plans and Other Illustrations* (Mount Vernon: MVLA, 1960).

21. Gardener's Report, MVLA Minutes, 1893, 69.

22. Report of Gardener, MVLA Minutes, 1905, 41.

23. Report of the Flower Garden Committee, MVLA Minutes, 1934, 66.

24. [Harold T. Abbott,] Report of Landscape Architect, MVLA Minutes, 1935, 30.

25. J. Dean Norton and Susanne A. Schrage-Norton, "The Upper Garden at Mount Vernon Estate, Its Past, Present, and Future: A Reflection of 18th-Century Gardening. Phase II: The Complete Report, 1985," unpublished report, on file, Historic Preservation Office, MVLA.

26. Clara S. McCarty, *The Story of Boxwood* (Richmond, Va.: Dietz Press, 1950).

27. Regent's Report, MVLA Minutes, 1900, 15.

28. Garden and Greenhouse Committee Report, MVLA Minutes, 1907, 49.

29. Quoted in Edward C. Carter II and Angeline Polites, eds., *The Virginia Journals of Benjamin Henry Latrobe, 1795–1798*, 2 vols. (New Haven, Conn.: Yale University Press for the Maryland Historical Society, 1977), 1: 165.

## "Laid Out in Squares, and Boxed with Great Precission": *Uncovering George Washington's Upper Garden*

The quotation used in the title is from Benjamin Henry Latrobe's description of his July 1796 visit to Mount Vernon, in Edward C. Carter II and Angeline Polites, eds., *The Virginia Journals of Benjamin Henry Latrobe, 1795–1798*, 2 vols. (New Haven, Conn.: Yale University Press for the Maryland Historical Society, 1977), 1: 165

1. The research program is detailed in Esther C. White and Curt Breckenridge, "'Gardens abounding in much gay and Vari[e]gated Foliage': Understanding George Washington's Upper Garden," *Magnolia* 23, no. 2 (Spring 2010): 1–6; and Dennis J. Pogue, "Restoring the Upper Garden: Original Designs, Both Complex and Interesting," MVLA AR, 2011, 24–39.

2. Dennis J. Pogue, J. Dean Norton, and Esther C. White, "Mount Vernon Upper Garden Restoration Research Design," unpublished report, Sept. 27, 2007; on file, Historic Preservation Office, MVLA.

3. Susan Buck to Dennis J. Pogue, "Boxwood rings photography," memorandum, Feb. 14, 2009; on file, Historic Preservation Office, MVLA.

4. Entry for Mar. 21, 1763, GWD, 1: 315.

5. Memoranda for Mar. 10 and 11, 1775, GWD, 3: 319.

6. GW to Lund Washington, Aug. 19, 1776, PGW Digital.

7. See entries for Jan. 12, Feb. 22, Mar. 7, 11, 12, 24, 29, Apr. 12, 1785, and Apr. 6, 1786, GWD, 4: 75, 94, 99, 100, 101, 107, 109, 117.

8. Lund Washington to GW, Nov. 12, 1775, PGW Digital.

9. Samuel Vaughan, Journal, June 18–Sept. 4, 1787, and Vaughan presentation drawing of Mount Vernon, 1787, both Smith Library, Mount Vernon.

10. For visitors' accounts, see Jean B. Lee, ed., *Experiencing Mount Vernon: Eyewitness Accounts, 1784–1865* (Charlottesville: University of Virginia Press, 2006).

11. Winthrop Sargent, entry for Oct. 13, 1793, Diary, Oct. 1, 1793–Dec. 31, 1795, Winthrop Sargent Papers, Massachusetts Historical Society; quoted in editorial note 4, GW to James Madison, Oct. 14, 1793, PGW Digital.

12. Quoted in Carter and Polites, eds., *Virginia Journals of Benjamin Henry Latrobe*, 1: 165.

13. Thomas Mawe and John Abercrombie, *The Universal Gardener and Botanist; or, a General Dictionary of Gardening and Botany* (London: Printed for G. Robinson et al., 1778).

14. See, for example, Charles Herman Ruggles to Sarah C. Ruggles, Apr. 28, 1822, Washington Collection, Smith Library, Mount Vernon.

15. Both hired white gardeners and enslaved ones tended Mount Vernon's gardens over the years. For Washington's hired gardeners, see Adam Erby, "Designing the Beautiful: General Washington's Landscape Improvements, 1784–1787," this book, 28, 31–32. Documentation of the enslaved gardeners is in Weekly Plantation Reports, January 1797–January 1799; transcript on file, Historic Preservation Office, MVLA. For the nineteenth-century enslaved gardeners, see Lee, ed., *Experiencing Mount Vernon*; and Scott E. Casper, *Sarah Johnson's Mount Vernon* (New York: Hill and Wang, 2008).

16. Quoted in Lee, ed., *Experiencing Mount Vernon*, 141.

17. The idea that George Washington personally planted items in the upper garden seems to have originated in the 1820s and to have grown strong after that decade. In 1822 Massachusetts U.S. Senator Elijah H. Mills was among

the first to suggest that Washington personally designed it; see Mills to Harriet Blake Mills, Jan. 22, 1822, in *Proceedings of the Massachusetts Historical Society* 19 (1881–1882), 34; also transcribed in "Our Gardens as They Were and Now, 1858–1941," research paper, circa 1951, in Gardens and Greenhouses, Black Notebook Collection, no. 21, Smith Library, Mount Vernon. By the time of Caroline Moore's visit in 1833, such accounts had become quite common.

18. Gardiner Hallock, "Pisé Construction in Early Nineteenth-Century Virginia," *Perspectives in Vernacular Architecture* 11 (2004): 40–53.

19. Bushrod's garden structures are identified and located in Bushrod Washington to James Rawlings, Aug. 8, 1815, manuscript collection, Smith Library, Mount Vernon.

20. Memorandum, Green House Plants, June 14, 1833, in Notes and Abstracts from a Calf Bound Volume containing the Diary of John A. Washington, 1810–1842, Smith Library, Mount Vernon.

21. Lee, ed., *Experiencing Mount Vernon*, 151–57.

22. Two letters note the early work in the upper garden: George W. Riggs to Ann Pamela Cunningham, July 25, 1859, and Upton Herbert to Ann Pamela Cunningham, Aug. 18, 1859, both Smith Library, Mount Vernon. The seed house was restored, repairs were made to the garden walls and wooden paling, and the paths were found and re-graveled.

23. James Craig to Hon. N. N. Halsted, "three greenhouses nearly roofed," June 25, 1869, archives collection, Smith Library, Mount Vernon.

24. Woodrow Wilson, "First in Peace," *Harper's New Monthly Magazine* 93, no. 556 (Sept. 1896): 488 (frontispiece); Howard Pyle to Woodrow Wilson, Mar. 27, 1896, *The Papers of Woodrow Wilson*, Arthur S. Link, ed., vol. 9, 1894–96 (Princeton: Princeton University Press, 1970), 493.

25. Ibid., vol. 10, 1896–98, 64–68, repr. William Milligan Sloane, "Review of *George Washington*," *New York Book Buyer* 13 (Dec. 1896): 724–29.

26. Walter Macomber, "The Rebuilding of the Greenhouse-Quarters," MVLA AR, 1953, 19–27.

27. J. Dean Norton and Susanne A. Schrage-Norton, "The Upper Garden at Mount Vernon Estate, Its Past, Present, and Future: A Reflection of 18th-Century Gardening. Phase II: The Complete Report, 1985," unpublished report, on file, Historic Preservation Office, MVLA.

28. Batty Langley, *New Principles of Gardening; or, The Laying out and Planting of Parterres, Groves, Wildernesses, Labyrinths,* *Avenues, Parks, &c.* (London: Printed for A. Bettesworth and J. Batley, 1728).

29. John E. Latta, entry for July 3, 1799, "Visit to Mount Vernon in 1799," paper read to the Bucks County, Pennsylvania, Historical Society, n.d.; transcribed in Early Descriptions of Mount Vernon, 1800–1841, vol. 1, Black Notebook Collection, no. 16, Smith Library, Mount Vernon. Weekly reports of George Washington's gardener, Jan. 7, 1797–Jan. 26, 1799, unpublished transcript, Smith Library, Mount Vernon.

30. Quoted in Carter and Polites, eds., *Virginia Journals of Benjamin Henry Latrobe*, 1: 165.

### GARDENS AND GROVES: *A Landscape Guide*

1. Dennis J. Pogue, "Approaching Mount Vernon," unpublished research report, n.d., revised Mar. 3, 2010; on file, Historic Preservation Office, MVLA.

2. Quoted in Edward C. Carter II and Angeline Polites, eds., *The Virginia Journals of Benjamin Henry Latrobe, 1795–1798*, 2 vols. (New Haven, Conn.: Yale University Press for the Maryland Historical Society, 1977), 1: 165.

3. For a detailed discussion of the view of the Potomac River from the Mansion's piazza, see Joseph Manca, *George Washington's Eye: Landscape, Architecture, and Design at Mount Vernon* (Baltimore: Johns Hopkins University Press, 2012), 155–61.

4. Louis-Philippe d'Orléans, *Journal de mon voyage d'Amerique*, ed. Suzanne d'Huart (Paris: Flammarion, 1976), 53–55, quoted in Manca, *George Washington's Eye*, 98.

5. GW to Clement Biddle, Nov. 4, 1784, PGW Digital.

6. Clement Biddle to GW, Jan. 29, 1785, PGW Digital.

7. On the evolution of grass cutting, see Anthony Huxley, *An Illustrated History of Gardening* (New York: Lyons Press, 1998), 279–81.

8. Julian Ursyn Niemcewicz, *Under Their Vine and Fig Tree: Travels through America in 1797–1799, 1805, with Some Further Account of Life in New Jersey*, trans. and ed. Metchie J. E. Budka (Elizabeth, N.J.: Grassmann Publishing, 1965), 98. Niemcewicz's diary contains an extensive description of the many flowering shrubs and trees he saw at Mount Vernon.

9. For a detailed description of the bowling green as the central element of this part of the landscape, see Manca, *George Washington's Eye*, 97–104.

10. For a detailed description, see Dennis J. Pogue, "Restoring

the Upper Garden: Original Designs, Both Complex and Interesting," MVLA AR, 2011, 25–39.

11. James Taylor, entry for spring 1805, transcribed in "Passage from the 'Narrative of General James Taylor of Newport, Kentucky,'" in Early Descriptions of Mount Vernon, 1800–1841, vol. 1, Black Notebook Collection, no. 16, Smith Library, Mount Vernon.

12. Quoted in Carter and Polites, eds., *Virginia Journals of Benjamin Henry Latrobe*, 1: 165.

13. John E. Latta, entry for July 3, 1799, "Visit to Mount Vernon in 1799," paper read to the Bucks County, Pennsylvania, Historical Society, n.d.

14. Niemcewicz, *Under Their Vine and Fig Tree*, 97.

15. GW to Tench Tilghman, Aug. 11, 1784, and Tench Tilghman to GW, Aug. 18 1784, PGW Digital.

16. Manca, *George Washington's Eye*, 32.

17. George Washington, Memorandum and sketch of greenhouse and quarters, circa 1785, W-799, Smith Library, Mount Vernon; George Augustine Washington to GW, Apr. 15, 1792, PGW Digital.

18. Dennis J. Pogue, "Restoring the Greenhouse Slave Quarters," MVLA AR, 2010, 35–43.

19. Both documents are in the Mutual Assurance Society of Virginia, Business Records Collection (accession no. 301770), Library of Virginia, Richmond. The 1803 version was drawn by Lewis M. Rivalain and is contained in vol. 26. The second document was drawn by Samuel Lewis and F. Hamersley and is policy no. 18, vol. 35.

20. Thomas Mawe and John Abercrombie, *The Universal Gardener and Botanist; or, a General Dictionary of Gardening and Botany* (London: Printed for G. Robinson et al., 1778), s.v. "Kitchen-garden."

21. Evelyn Acomb, "The Journal of Baron von Closen," *William and Mary Quarterly*, 3rd ser., 10, no. 2 (Apr. 1953): 229.

22. For more on the lower garden, see J. Dean Norton, "'An abundance of every thing': Mount Vernon's Fruit and Vegetable Gardens," in Stephen A. McLeod, ed., *Dining with the Washingtons: Historic Recipes, Entertainment, and Hospitality from Mount Vernon* (Mount Vernon: MVLA, 2011), 79–83.

23. Martha Washington to Frances (Fanny) Bassett Washington, July 1, 1792, in *"Worthy Partner": The Papers of Martha Washington*, comp. Joseph E. Fields (Westport, Conn.: Greenwood Press, 1994), 239.

24. Amariah Frost diary, quoted in Moncure D. Conway, "Footprints in Washingtonland," *Harper's New Monthly Magazine* 78, no. 467 (Apr. 1889): 743.

25. GW to Anthony Whitting, Feb. 3, 1793, PGW Digital.

26. Entry for July 8, 1785, GWD, 4: 161–62.

27. Entry for Nov. 14, 1785, GWD, 4: 222–23.

28. GW to Benjamin Fitzhugh Grymes, Mar. 16, 1786, PGW Digital.

29. Gregory A. Stiverson and Patrick H. Butler III, eds., "Virginia in 1732: The Travel Journal of William Hugh Grove," *Virginia Magazine of History and Biography* 85, no. 1 (Jan. 1977): 18–44.

30. For plantation outbuildings, see John Michael Vlach, *Back of the Big House: The Architecture of Plantation Slavery* (Chapel Hill: University of North Carolina Press, 1993).

31. Dennis J. Pogue, "Mount Vernon: Transformation of an Eighteenth-Century Plantation System," in Paul A. Shackel and Barbara J. Little, eds., *Historical Archaeology of the Chesapeake* (Washington, D.C.: Smithsonian Institution Press, 1994), 101–14.

32. Entry for Sept. 30, 1785, GWD 4: 199.

33. For a concise explanation of the role of deer parks in British country estates, see Charles Quest-Ritson, *The English Garden: A Social History* (Boston: David R. Godine, 2001), 28–32.

34. Benjamin Ogle to GW, Aug. 20, 1785, PGW Digital.

35. Benjamin Ogle to GW, July 12, 1786, PGW Digital.

36. GW to George William Fairfax, June 25, 1786; GW to Doddridge Pitt Chichester and Daniel McCarty Chichester, Apr. 25, 1799, PGW Digital.

37. GW to William Pearce, Dec. 28, 1794, PGW Digital.

38. GW to Richard Chichester, Aug. 8, 1792; GW to Doddridge Pitt Chichester and Daniel McCarty Chichester, Apr. 25, 1799, PGW Digital.

39. Richard Chichester to GW, Nov. 10, 1793, PGW Digital.

## PLANT LISTS

1. William Hamilton to GW, Mar. 17, 1792, PGW Digital. The list is transcribed from "List of Plants, from Mr. Hamilton's" [Mar. 1792], PGW Digital. The original document is docketed in George Washington's hand, "List of Plants & Shrubs from Mr. Bartram March 1792," and it is attached to another plant list, which is entitled, "Catalogue of Trees, Shrubs & Plants of Jno Bartram." Both documents are preserved at the Library of Congress, George Washington Papers, 1741–1799: Series 4. General Correspondence, 1697–1799, with a digitized version online.

2. The list is transcribed from "Catalogue of Trees, Shrubs & Plants of Jno Bartram—March 1792," PGW Digital. The original document is attached to a "List of Plants, from Mr. Hamilton's," which is docketed in George Washington's hand, "List of Plants & Shrubs from Mr. Bartram March 1792." Both documents are preserved at the Library of Congress, George Washington Papers, 1741–1799: Series 4. General Correspondence, 1697–1799, with a digitized version online. Letter codes for recommended soil type and growing heights, provided in original document, are not included here.

   Plant names for this list and the following list are derived as follows:
   - [Names in brackets] are as supplied in PGW Digital.
   - (Common names in parenthesis) are as given by Bartram in the original list.
   - "Common names in quotations" are as given for corresponding plants in William Bartram, "Catalogue of American Trees, Shrubs, and Herbacious Plants" (Philadelphia, 1784). This broadside advertised seeds and plants available for purchase from the Bartram nursery.
   - All other common names are as supplied in PGW Digital.

   For further notes on plant classifications, see the document in PGW Digital; also Joel T. Fry, "Bartram's Garden Catalogue of North American Plants, 1783," *Journal of Garden History* 16, no. 1 (Jan.–Mar. 1996): 1–66.

3. George Augustine Washington to GW, Apr. 8–9, 1792, PGW Digital.

4. This information is courtesy of Joel T. Fry, Curator, Bartram's Garden, Philadelphia.

5. George Augustine Washington to GW, Apr. 8–9, 1792, PGW Digital.

6. Transcribed from "Directive to John Christian Ehlers, November 7, 1792," PGW Digital. The original list is titled "List of Trees, Shrubs &c. had of Jno. Bartram to supply the place of those of his Catalogue of Mar: 92. which failed." The manuscript is preserved at the Library of Congress, George Washington Papers, 1741–1799. Formatting of plant names and common names is the same as on the preceding list; see note 2, above.

7. Ibid. Washington's instructions are titled "Directions for disposing of the Trees, Shrubs &ca, mentioned in the aforegoing list."

8. List compiled by Mount Vernon archaeology staff. George Washington's references from PGW Digital, plus the weekly reports submitted by his gardener and farm manager, Weekly Plantation Reports, January 1797–January 1799; transcript on file, Historic Preservation Office, MVLA. For relevant visitors' accounts, see: Benjamin Henry Latrobe, quoted in Edward C. Carter II and Angeline Polites, eds., *The Virginia Journals of Benjamin Henry Latrobe, 1795–1798*, 2 vols. (New Haven, Conn.: Yale University Press for the Maryland Historical Society, 1977), 1: 165; Julian Ursyn Niemcewicz, *Under Their Vine and Fig Tree: Travels through America in 1797–1799, 1805, with Some Further Account of Life in New Jersey*, trans. and ed. Metchie J. E. Budka (Elizabeth, N.J.: Grassmann Publishing, 1965), 97–98; Amariah Frost diary, quoted in Moncure D. Conway, "Footprints in Washingtonland," *Harper's New Monthly Magazine* 78, no. 467 (Apr. 1889): 743; and John E. Latta, entry for July 3, 1799, "Visit to Mount Vernon in 1799," paper read to the Bucks County, Pennsylvania, Historical Society, n.d.

9. Common and scientific names listed here were supplied by the horticulture staff, George Washington's Mount Vernon.

# Further Reading

Cadou, Carol Borchert. *The George Washington Collection: Fine and Decorative Arts at Mount Vernon*. Manchester, Vt.: Hudson Hills Press, 2006.

Dalzell, Robert F., Jr., and Lee Baldwin Dalzell. *George Washington's Mount Vernon: At Home in Revolutionary America*. New York: Oxford University Press, 1998.

Favretti, Rudy J., and Joy Putman Favretti. *Landscapes and Gardens for Historic Buildings*. 2nd ed., rev. Nashville, Tenn.: American Association for State and Local History, 1991.

de Forest, Elizabeth Kellam. *The Gardens and Grounds at Mount Vernon: How George Washington Planned and Planted Them*. Mount Vernon, Va.: Mount Vernon Ladies' Association of the Union, 1982.

Fry, Joel T. "Bartram's Garden Catalogue of North American Plants, 1783." *Journal of Garden History* 16, no. 1 (Jan.–Mar. 1996): 1–66.

Garrett, Wendell, ed. *George Washington's Mount Vernon*. New York: Monacelli Press, 1998.

Greenberg, Allan. *George Washington, Architect*. London: Andreas Papadakis, 1999.

Griswold, Mac. *Washington's Gardens at Mount Vernon: Landscape of the Inner Man*. Boston: Houghton Mifflin, 1999.

Hunt, John Dixon. *The Picturesque Garden in Europe*. London: Thames and Hudson, 2002.

Lee, Jean B., ed. *Experiencing Mount Vernon: Eyewitness Accounts, 1784–1865*. Charlottesville: University of Virginia Press, 2006.

Leighton, Ann. *American Gardens in the Eighteenth Century: "For Use or for Delight."* Amherst: University of Massachusetts Press, 1986.

Manca, Joseph. *George Washington's Eye: Landscape, Architecture, and Design at Mount Vernon*. Baltimore: Johns Hopkins University Press, 2012.

Martin, Peter. *The Pleasure Gardens of Virginia: From Jamestown to Jefferson*. Princeton, N.J.: Princeton University Press, 1991.

Norton, J. Dean. "Restoring Mount Vernon's Gardens and Landscapes." In Stephen A. McLeod, ed. *The Mount Vernon Ladies' Association: 150 Years of Restoring George Washington's Home*. Mount Vernon, Va.: Mount Vernon Ladies' Association, 2010, 167–75.

Pogue, Dennis J. "Mount Vernon: Transformation of an Eighteenth-Century Plantation System." In Paul A. Shackel and Barbara J. Little, eds. *Historical Archaeology of the Chesapeake*. Washington, D.C.: Smithsonian Institution Press, 1994, 101–14.

Quest-Ritson, Charles. *The English Garden: A Social History*. Boston: David R. Godine, 2001.

Sarudy, Barbara Wells. *Gardens and Gardening in the Chesapeake, 1700–1805*. Baltimore: Johns Hopkins University Press, 1998.

Upton, Dell. "White and Black Landscapes in Eighteenth-Century Virginia." *Places* 2, no. 2 (1984): 59–72.

Vlach, John Michael. *Back of the Big House: The Architecture of Plantation Slavery*. Chapel Hill: University of North Carolina Press, 1993.

White, Esther C. and Curt Breckenridge. "'Gardens abounding in much gay and Vari[e]gated Foliage': Understanding George Washington's Upper Garden." *Magnolia* 23, no. 2 (Spring 2010): 1–6.

Wulf, Andrea. *Founding Gardeners: The Revolutionary Generation, Nature, and the Shaping of the American Nation*. New York: Alfred A. Knopf, 2011.

# Index to Text

This index includes individuals, organizations, places, books, and objects mentioned in the main text. For an index to the plant lists that follow the text, turn to page 183.

The names George and Martha Washington are abbreviated GW and MW. Mount Vernon is abbreviated MV. The Mount Vernon Ladies' Association is abbreviated MVLA.

Page numbers in *italics* indicate illustrations.

broccoli, 127
Buck, Susan, historic paint analyst, 72
building campaign, mid-1770s, 76
bust of GW (1785), by Jean-Antoine Houdon, frontispiece
Byrds, Tidewater, Virginia, estate, formal gardens, 5

# C

cabbage(s), 127, *128*
Canadian hemlock, 46
carriage circle, west side of Mansion, formal geometry of, 34
Carroll, Margaret Tilghman, 24, 25; greenhouse, 118; home of, Mount Clare, 24
Carter's Grove, Virginia plantation gardens at, 96
Carters, Tidewater, Virginia, estate of, formal gardens, 5
cauliflower, 127
century plant, admired by visitors to MV (c. 1859), *122*
Cheere, Sir Henry, designer of marble mantle (c. 1770) for Mansion "New Room," *33*
cherry trees: Black May Cherry, Cornation, May Cherry, May Duke, 75
chestnut oak, one of the oldest trees on MV estate, 46; swamp chestnut oak, 46, *108*
Chichester, Richard, neighbor of GW, 137
Chinese seeds, 130
chives, 127
chronology of paths, 96; curving, more stylish, 17; gravel(ed), uncovered by archaeologists, *81*, 82, 100; and increase in paths (1985), 95; "labyrinth of" in wilderness areas, 49; and MVLA task to restore, 90; upper garden, with 31 small beds and 24 paths (1985), 62, *63*; location and width confirmed by archaeology, *83*; lozenge-shaped, 95; and narrowing of, by plantings, 85, 95; number increased during Bushrod Washington's tenure, 89; plan to preserve wide paths, 99
Cincinnatus, ancient Roman statesman, xi, 95
cisterns, 50
Clinton, George, New York governor, 27–28
cold frames, 5
Colonial Williamsburg, 50
Constitutional Convention, Philadelphia (1787), beginning of, 3, 34; and GW, 32, 81
Continental Army, GW takes command of (June 1775), 12, 76; GW resigns commission (December 1783), 76
cowpeas, planting of, 61
crab apple(s), 12, 27, 76

Craik, Dr. James, friend of GW, and gift of Chinese seeds to, 130
cucumbers, 127
Cunningham, Ann Pamela, founding Regent, MVLA, xii, 39, 40
cupola atop Mansion (1787), 34, *35*; view from, 6

# D

dairy, 5
Dandridge, Bartholomew, Jr., nephew of MW, 155
death of GW (1799), 32, 34, 39, 45, 68, 72, 81, 85, 86
deer park, 18 acres on eastern slope, 137; images related to, *138–41*
deer, English, at Bell-Air, 137; from George William Fairfax, 137; at MV, tame and treated almost as pets, 137; prized buck killed by hunter (neighbor?), 137
dendrochronologists, team of, at MV (2005), 46
diary, entries on trees, by GW, 27, 28, 75
dill, 127
dogwood, 12, 27, 76
double digging, mixing and preparing soil for cultivation, *80*, 82
dung (fertilizer) repository, 133

# E

Edison, Thomas A., and installation of lightning rods on larger trees at MV, 46
Ehlers, Catherine, wife of John Christian Ehlers, 31
Ehlers, John Christian, gardener at MV, 31, 32, 155
English landscape: designers, 104; ideas for MV, 76
English or goose grass seed, 111
engraving, of MV's gardens, by Lossing, 18
enslaved: children at Mansion House Farm, 18, 32; cook(s), 32, 127; gardeners, 86, 99, 111, 127, 130; workers, brought to MV by Bushrod Washington, 86; workforce, 18, 27, 28, 32, 86, 104, 120. *See also* slave(s), slave quarter(s)
Erby, Adam, 76
espaliered fruit tree(s), 50, 61, 96, 114, *129, 164*

# F

Fairfax family, GW's surveying for, 24, 27
Fairfax, George William, GW's friend and neighbor, 137
Favretti, Rudy, landscape architect, 49
fig trees, 127

fire (1835), destroys GW's brick greenhouse, 89

Fisher, Robert B., MV horticulturist, 57; co-author, with Wall, "A List of Ornamental Trees and Shrubs Noted in the Writings of George Washington" (c. 1950), 57; revised and expanded MV's booklet *The Mount Vernon Gardens* (1960), 57

flower knots, planted in upper garden, 75

flowerpot fragments (18th-century) recovered in upper garden excavations, 84, 85

flower sales, at MV, 40

fringe trees, 12, 18

Frost, Amariah, Massachusetts preacher, 127, 160

fruit and nut nursery, 75

fruit trees: 50, 65, 96, 99, 100, 114; espaliered, 61, *129, 164*

fruits, mentioned by Niemcewicz in upper garden (1798): "Corrents, Rasberys, Strawberys, Gusberys, [and] quantities of peaches and cherries," 114

# G

Garden Club of Virginia, and plan for bowling green, 49

garden booklet, *The Mount Vernon Gardens* (c. 1941), by Harrison; revised (1960) by Fisher, 57

garden, experimental, at MV, 24, 130

*Gardener's Dictionary* (1731), by Miller, and abridged version (1763), copy owned by GW, 24

gardener's house, interior view, *31*

gardening manuals, 18th-century, mostly written by British authors, 24, 130

gardening texts, 18th-century, Mawe and Abercrombie's *Universal Gardener*, 85

gardens at MV: botanic gardens, 50; bullet-shaped, 17; fruit garden, 50, 61–62; kitchen garden, 5, 24, 31, 50, 54, 81, 82, *126*; MW involved in operations of, 127; plans for, 68; pleasure garden [or grounds], 5, 12, 17, 18, 24, 28, drawing by Vaughan, 34, ornamental trees at, 45, tours of, 31, 61, 99, 103, 111, 114; nursery, 27, 50, *60*, 61–62; fruit and nut, 75

gardens, formal American, of the late 18th century: Peyton Randolph House in Williamsburg, Virginia; William Paca House in Annapolis, Maryland; Virginia plantation gardens at Prestwould, Westover, Carter's Grove, Mount Pleasant, and Bacon's Castle: 96

geometrical layout, upper garden, 82

*George Washington as a Colonel in the Virginia Regiment* (1772), by Peale, *11*

*George Washington at Verplanck's Point* (1790), by John Trumbull, xiv, *xvi*

Georgian symmetry of Mansion, 8

goose grass seed, 111

grafting trees, 75

grapevines, 5

grasses, 57, 61

gravel from excavation of upper garden, hauled by slaves, *120*

*Great Double Daisy*, from William Curtis's *Botanical Magazine* (1794), *117*

*Great Falls of the Potomac, The* (c. 1797), by George Beck, *10, 11*

greenhouse complex/greenhouse slave quarter: drawing for, by GW (c. 1785), 120, *121*; drawing by Rivalain for Mutual Assurance Society of Virginia (1803), *121*; as socially divided space, 120

greenhouse, at Mount Clare, Carroll's home, as basis for the one at MV, 24

greenhouse, at MV: 28, 29, 40, 59, 67, 69, 73, 92, *115*, 118–35; *118, 119*; Bushrod Washington's pisé greenhouse, 86, drawing for, by GW (c. 1785), 120, *121*; catalog of plants for sale from (1882), 40, 42; completed (1787), 28; destroyed by fire (1835), 89, 120; interior view of (1987), *123*; large, of brick, 17, 71, 82, 114; Latrobe, comment on (1796), 82; new greenhouse (1869), 90; paths provide easy access to, 82, 85, 99, 100, 111; and pinery, 86; reconstructed by MVLA (1951), 95; in ruins, 89; ruins as romantic backdrop, 89, and as illustrated by Lossing (1859), *88*, 89; Winthrop Sargent, comment on (1793), 82. *See also* hothouse

gristmill, 27

Guinea grass, seeds of, from Barbados, brought by nephew, 130

# H

ha-ha, or walled ditch, 17, 104; aquatint by Parkyns (1799) showing ha-ha wall, 49; GW's drawing of (1798), *136*

Hamilton, William, 142, 143, 145

hanging wood, term used by English landscape designers, 104

*Harper's New Monthly Magazine* (1896), biographical sketches of GW by Wilson, 95

Harrison, Hetty Cary, MVLA Vice Regent for Virginia, 57

herb borders, 50

Herbert, Upton, MV's first resident superintendent, 40

herbs planted in lower garden, 127

Hercules, enslaved cook, 32

horse stalls, mucking out of, 133

*Horticulture*, magazine, 57

hothouse (greenhouse), added by Bushrod Washington, 86, 89

"house for families," slave quarter, 75

Mansion: as center of GW's pleasure grounds, 103; cupola as symbolic addition to (1787), 34; evolution of, and surrounding landscape during GW's lifetime, plans and elevations, 4; expansion, alterations, by GW, 5, 8, 12, 76; exterior and outbuildings, of wood, finished to look like stone, 133; MVLA decision to restore, 39; landscape work west of, 81; and outbuildings, 133; piazza and views, 104; and trinity of hallowed sites, 86; view of, cut off by wall, 12, 17

Mansion, views and images of: *x*, aerial view, *16*, *17*; bowling green and Mansion from the west, *vi*, vii, *14–15*, *102*, *111*, *162*; east facade, *106*; *East Front of Mount Vernon* (c. 1787–92), attrib. to Savage, *138*; east slope below Mansion, site of lost deer park, 139, *140–41*; view from lower garden, *134*; Mansion cupola and dove of peace weathervane, 34, *35*; view from outbuildings, *x*, *134*; *View of Mount Vernon Looking to the North* (1796), by Latrobe, *13*; *View of Mount Vernon with the Washington Family on the Piazza* (1796), by Latrobe, *107*, detail of (gatefold), *109*; *View of the Mansion from the West*, aquatint by Parkyns, *48–49*; *View to the North from the Lawn at Mount Vernon* (1796), by Latrobe, *104–5*

mantelpiece, marble, in Mansion "New Room," by Cheere, *33*; gift of Vaughan, 32

maple trees, 28

Mawe, Thomas, and John Abercrombie, *Universal Gardener and Botanist* (1778), 85

maze(s), boxwood, 85, 99

meat: butchering, 12; smoking, 12, 133

Miller, Philip, *Gardener's Dictionary* (1731), 24, 27; copy of abridged edition owned by GW, 24

Missisippi [*sic*] Nuts, 75

Montbrillant, royal gardens in Hanover, Germany, 31

Moore, Caroline, Bostonian, journal entry re: visit to MV, 86

Mount Clare, home of Carroll, outside Baltimore, 24

Mount Pleasant, Virginia plantation gardens at, 96

*Mount Vernon and Its Associations: Historical, Biographical, and Pictorial* (1859), by Lossing, 17

*Mount Vernon Gardens, The* (c. 1941), booklet by Harrison, 57

Mount Vernon Ladies' Association (MVLA), 90–95; boxwood as plant most often mentioned in records of, 62; committee on gardens and greenhouses, 40, 65; kitchen garden committee, 50, and task to restore paths, 90; and reconstruction of greenhouse (1951), unveiled restored upper garden (2011), 71

mulberries: English, 127; white, 46

Mutual Assurance Society of Virginia: drawing of MV greenhouse (1803) by Rivalain, *121*

N

naturalistic gardening, Langley's book one of the first written on, 5

naturalistic landscape, meant to be explored and enjoyed, 100; remodeling of upper garden to, 82

"A Neat Landskip," after Claude Lorrain, purchased by GW for Mansion west parlor, 8, 9

"necessaries" (outhouses), 12, 14, 75

neighbors of GW: Chichester and Fairfax, 137

"new garden," GW's term for upper garden, 75

"New Room" mantle in Mansion, designed by Cheere (c. 1770), *33*

*New Principles of Gardening* (1728), by Langley, 5, 24, 25, 63, 95

Niemcewicz, Julian Ursyn, Polish nobleman, visitor to MV, 3, 160; quote re: "all the vegetables for the kitchen, Corrents, Rasberys, Strawberys, Gusberys, [and] quantities of peaches and cherries," 114

Norton, J. Dean, MV horticulturist, and Schrage, research and report on upper garden (1985), 58; and proposed alterations to rose gardens, 61

nursery beds, *60*

O

octagonal houses, as tool sheds, 75, 85

Ogle, Benjamin, friend of GW, 137; and home, Bell-Air, near Annapolis, 137

oranges: for MW's table, 118; served to guests at MV, 127; sweet and bitter, among plants cultivated at MV after Bushrod Washington's death, 89

orchard, 85, 96

ornamental flowers/plants, 17, 61, 96, 111

ornamental trees/shrubs, 45, 114, 145; "A List of Ornamental Trees and Shrubs Noted in the Writings of George Washington" (c. 1950), by Fisher and Wall, 57

outbuildings, *x*, 6, *132*, 133–35; arrangement of, when GW took over MV (1754), 5; and MVLA, 39; MV's existing, razed (1775), 8; on south work lane, 6, 132; straight lines of, 34; trees to be planted to block view of, 12; and GW's plans to reorganize, 76. *See also* greenhouse, gristmill, hothouse, wash house

ovals, part of GW's landscape plan for MV, 49, 155

# P

Paca, William, House, Annapolis, Maryland, 96

Parkyns, George Isham (1749–1820), aquatint view of Mansion from the west (1799), *48–49*

parterre, *xiv*, *xv*, 99, 114; comment by Latrobe, 82

paths: 18th-century paths restored in 2010, 65, 66; alignment of 1790 paths with Vaughan's 1787 drawing, 85; archaeology to discover 18th-century paths and beds, 58, *80*, *81*, 85; between groupings of young trees, 65; along carriage way, 12; in upper garden, covered with wooden planking (1899–1902), 90, *91*

peach(es): 75, 114; Kernals [*sic*], 75

Peale, Charles Willson (1741–1827), first known portrait of GW (1772), 8, *11*; portrait of William Bartram (1808), *150*; portrait of Margaret Tilghman Carroll (1770–71), *25*; portrait miniature of MW (1772), *129*

peas, 127; cowpeas, 61

Philadelphia Society for Promoting Agriculture, 32

piazza (of Mansion), and views from, 106; *View of Mount Vernon with the Washington Family on the Piazza* (1796), by Latrobe, 106, *107*, gatefold *109*

picturesque landscape(s), 8, 76, 82, 100

"pine labyrinths," along serpentine path, 28, 111

Pine, Robert Edge (1730–1788), 32; portrait of Vaughan (1760), *33*

pine trees, 27

pinery, greenhouse for growing pineapples, 86, 89

pisé, rammed-earth structure, 86, 89

*Plan of Mount Vernon* (1859), published by Lossing, 22

plank walkways, 90

plant list(s), from John Bartram's nursery: March 1792, 145, *147*; November 1792, 155, *156*; in Fisher's revision of *The Mount Vernon Gardens* (1960), 57; from William Hamilton, March 1792, *143*; Schrage's (1982), 57; "Trees, Shrubs, and Vines," 161; "Upper Garden Plants," 161. *See also* Index to Plant Lists

pleasure grounds: 18, complexity of GW's design for, 24; curving gravel walkway through, 111; designed by GW (1784–85), 24; for enjoyment of family and guests, 5, 61, 103, 114; Mansion as center of, 103; reproduced in Lossing's book, 17; as separate from working plantation, 17, 18; view of outbuildings shielded from, 133

poplar trees: to be planted by Lund Washington at MV, 12; tulip poplar, 26, 27; annual inspection of, *46*; Mansion seen from, *44*; pair of, at garden gates, 46

Porter, Thomas, Alexandria merchant, gift of Chinese seeds, 130

post holes, remaining from post-and-rail fence, 62

Potomac River, and access to MV by boat, 103; *The Great Falls of the Potomac River* (c. 1797), by Beck, *11*; views of, at MV, 12, 24, 27, 34, *108*; gravel hauled from, by slaves, *120*

Prestwould, Virginia plantation gardens at, 96

purple beech trees, 45

Pyle, Howard (1853–1911), artist, 90; frontispiece to Wilson's book *First in Peace*, 95; *Washington in the Garden at Mount Vernon*, 90, 94

# R

raisins, 127

Rakestraw, Joseph, house carpenter, 34; dove of peace weathervane by, *38*

Randolph, Peyton, gardens at house of, Williamsburg, Virginia, 96

Randolphs, Tidewater, Virginia estate of, formal gardens, 5

Revolutionary War, 3; expansion of MV before the war, 8, 12

Rivalain, Lewis M., 120

rose garden(s), Victorian, created by MVLA, 95; removed from MV, 61, 95

rose growers, Washington, D.C., 40

roses, exotic, 99; grown by MVLA, 90

royal gardens at Montbrillant, owned by King George III, 31

*Ruins of the Conservatory and Servants' Quarters* (1859), by Lossing, *88*, 89

rustication, method used to give rough appearance to building surfaces, 133

# S

sago palm, 86, 118, *122*, *123*

sales catalog, first (1882), MV garden and greenhouse, *42*, 90

salt house, 133

Sargent, Charles Sprague, director of Arnold Arboretum, Harvard University, and care of MV trees, 45; author, "The Trees of Mount Vernon" (1917), 45; diagram of trees near Mansion (1926), *47*

Sargent, Winthrop, on "Kitchen and Flower Gardens" and visitor to MV, 82

Sasafras [*sic*] (sassafras), 12

Savage, Edward (1761–1817), attrib. to: *East Front of Mount Vernon* (c. 1787–92), showing deer park, *138*; *West Front of Mount Vernon* (c. 1787–92), *112–13*

Schrage, Susanne, landscape historian and former Virginia Tech student, horticulture research on botanical garden by,

upper garden, *xv*, 58–61, *63*, 65–70, 71–102, *98*, 114–17; 18th-century flowerpot fragments recovered in excavations of, *84*; archaeology in, 96–100; boxwood parterre in, xiv, *xv*; boxwood planted in (1798), 62, overgrown along center path, 62; dwarf boxwood edging a floral border in (2013), *116*; enclosed by rectangular brick wall, 12; excavation at junction of main north-south and east-west paths (2009), *83*; excavation of western end (2009), *70*; gate to, 46; graveled paths marked on Vaughan's drawing of (1787), *80*, *81*; greenhouse as centerpiece of, 17; MVLA removed greenhouses from, 95; layout of (1985), 62; lists of plants in, based on GW's and visitors' accounts, 160; more ornamental than lower garden, 17; naturalistic principles not used in, 100; plan by Bailey (1940), *64*; paths covered with wooden planking (1899–1902), *90*, *91*; postcard views of: (c. 1900), *38* (1926), *59*; restoration of (2011); restoration plan for (2010), *64*, *65*; rose house built at east end of (1888), 40; scale model used to plan 2010 restoration of, *96*, *97*; stereoscopic view of (before 1881), MV employee at gate of, *92*; and trinity of hallowed MV sites, 86; and greenhouse (2013), 72, *73*; upper garden, greenhouse, and one slave quarter wing (2012), *118*; vegetables: planted in, *30*, introduced to, 95; view of (1970s), *41*; view from the northwest (2014), 76, *78–79*; views of (2012), *98*, *101*; wall, 46; GW in upper garden as frontispiece to *First in Peace*, *94*, 95; Whelan, MVLA's gardener, near rose beds, 92, *93*

## V

Vaughan drawings, by Samuel Vaughan, 2, 32, 34, *37*, 76, *77*; graveled paths on, *80*, *81*, *85*; as important document for restoration of upper garden, 81; shows three primary axial paths, *85*; upper garden recorded as kitchen garden in, 82

Vaughan, Samuel (1720–1802), friend of GW, 32, 81; journal, with sketch of MV landscape, 2, *36*; portrait of (1760), by Pine, *33*

vegetable beds: from 1770s, as record of archaeological features, 96; herb-bordered, 50; linear, 75; pleasure garden as border surrounding, 65

vegetables, 5, *31*; archaeology of long trenches, believed to be beds for vegetables planted in 1770s, 1780s, *74*; bordered with flowers, fruit trees, shrubs, 65, 75; flower border surrounding rows of vegetables (2013), *115*; gardener's weekly report focused on, 61, 96, 127; included in meals served at MV, 127; "little garden" and, 57; Bateman, and production of, 28; planted in "pleasure garden," 99; planted in former

east rose garden and "Vineyard Inclosure," 61; planted in interiors/centers of beds, 96, 99, 114; planted in lower garden, 127; planted in upper garden, *30*, 75; planted with flowers, fruit trees, and shrubs, 96, 100; reintroduced to upper garden, 95; rows of, in center of ornamental garden, 17, in center of kitchen garden, 50. *See also* artichokes, broccoli, cabbage, cauliflower, cucumbers, lettuce, peas

*View of Mount Vernon Looking to the North* (1796), by Latrobe, *13*

*View of Mount Vernon with the Washington Family on the Piazza* (1796), by Latrobe, *106–7*; detail of (gatefold), *109*

*View to the North from the Lawn at Mount Vernon* (1796), by Latrobe, *104–5*

"Vineyard Inclosure," converted to fruit garden and nursery, 61

visitors to MV, accounts by, 40, 58, 86, 96, 160

visto [vista], so-called by GW, 103

## W

walkways, arcaded, *6–7*, 8

Wall, Charles Cecil, MV's assistant resident superintendent, 50, resident director (1950), 57; co-author, with Fisher, "A List of Ornamental Trees and Shrubs Noted in the Writings of George Washington" (c. 1950), 57; and Williams, plan for lower garden (1937), 50

walled gardens flanking bowling green, 12, 17, 71

wash house/washing laundry, 133

Washington, Bushrod (1762–1829): GW's nephew and heir, 86; constructed three buildings at upper garden, 86; death of (1829), 89; increase in number of paths during tenure of, 89; and upper garden, 86

Washington, Fanny Bassett, niece of MW, 127

*Washington the Farmer*, illustration from *Life of George Washington* (1856), by Joel T. Headley, 86, *87*

Washington, George Augustine, GW's nephew and MV farm manager, 120, 155; gift of Guinea grass from Barbados, 130

Washington, George, drawing and description of ha-ha wall to replace deer park (1798), *136*; drawing for possible layout of greenhouse and slave quarter wings (c. 1785), *121*; survey of MV's five farms (1793), *20–21*

*Washington in the Garden at Mount Vernon*, by Pyle, 90, *94*

Washington, Jane Blackburn (tenure: 1832–41), widow of Bushrod's nephew and heir, John Augustine Washington II, 89

Washington, John Augustine II (tenure: 1829–32), 89

Washington, Lawrence, elder half-brother of GW, 5

# Index to Plant Lists

The plants itemized here appear in the Plant Lists (pages 143–61). Plants discussed or mentioned in the rest of the book are listed in the Index to Text (pages 174–82).

This index is divided into two lists, the first containing common plant names and the second containing Latin-based names.

Raspberry/raspberries, 160; flowering; thimbleberry (*Rubus odoratus*), 152, 158; flowering, twice-bearing, 143
Red bay, bay laurel, sweet bay (*Laurus nobilis*), 153, 158
Red buckeye (*Æsculus pavia*), 158
Redbud (*Cercis canadensis*), 161
Rhamnus (*Rhamnus alaternus*), 161; trees (buckthorn), 160
Rhododendron, or mountain rose laurel, 144
Roan tree, or mountain ash, 143
Rose Acacia, 143
Rose Laurel, sweet bay, swamp magnolia (*Magnolia glauca* [*Magnolia virginiana*]), 152
Roses, 160

## S

Sandbox tree (*Hura crepitans*), 161
Sassafras (*Sassafras albidum*), 161
Savin (*Juniperus sabina*), 151, 158
Scarlet Alpine strawberry seeds, 160
Scarlet rosemallow (*Hibiscus coccineus*), 153
Scotch fir (*Pinus communis*), 157
Seedgrass, 160
Service tree [prob.] (*Sorbus sativa* [prob. *Sorbus domestica*]), 148, 157
Shaddocks (lime, lemon), 160
Silk vine (*Periploca graeca*), 153
Simlens, 160
Snow-drop tree, Snowbell, storax (*Styrax grandifolium*), 148, 157
Sower orange, 160
Spanish dagger (*Yucca gloriosa*), 151
Spindle tree (*Evonimus americanus* [*Euonymus americanus*]), 151
Spirea frutex, 143
Spruce (*Picea glauca*), 161
Stewartia, or stuartia, silky (*Stewartia malachodendron*), 148, 157
St. John's wort (*H*[*ypericum*] *Angustifolium*), 145; shrub (*Hypericum kalmianum*), 143, 145, 155
St Peters wort, 143
Strawberries, 160
Sumac (*Rhus Italicum*), 152
Swamp red-berry bush (*Ilex verticillata*), 161
swamp rose (*Rosa Pennsylvanica flor: pleno* [*Rosa palustris*]), 152
Sweetbriar (*Rosa eglanteria*), 161
Sweet shrub of Carolina, Carolina allspice (*Calycanthus floridus*), 145, 155

Sycamore: oriental; oriental plane (*Platanus orientalis*), 151; (*Platanus occidentalis*), 161

## T

Thorn: large-berried (*Crataegus punctata*), 161; small-berried (*Crataegus spathulata*), 161
Thyme-leaved kalmia, lambkill, sheep laurel (*Kalmia angustifolia*) with the *Gaultheria* [*procumbens*], or mountain tea [wintergreen]), 146, 157

## U

Umbrella tree (*Magnolia tripetala*), 146

## V

*Viburnum opulifolium*, 146
Virginia sweetspire, Virginia willow, tasselwhite (*Itea virginiana* [*or virginica*]), 152

## W

Walnuts: English, French, 160
White pine (*Pinus Strobus*), 149, 157
Willow: with bay leaves, 143; bay leafed, 144; flowering, or palm, 144; with variegated leaves, 143; variegated, 144; silver blotched (*Salix variegata*), 151; weeping (*Salix babylonica*), 161; yellow (*Salix alba vitellina*), 161

## Y

Yellow root, in Carola (*Zanthorhiza apiifolia* [*Xanthorhiza simplicissima*]), 146
Yew: (*Taxus baccata*), 161; (*Taxus procumbens*), 145, 155

### Latin-based Plant Names

## A

*Acer*: *glaucum* [*Acer saccharinum*], silver-leafed maple, 148; *platanoides*, Norway maple, 148; *pumilum*; *s, montanum*, dwarf maple, 152, 158; *rubrum*, maple, 161; *sacharinum* [*Acer saccharum*], sugar maple, 148; *striatum* [*Acer pensylvanicum*], striped maple, moosewood, 148

*Æsculus: alba*, 151, 158; *hippocastanum*, horse chestnut, 146, 155; *pavia*, red buckeye, 149, 158; *varietas*, 151; *virginica*, yellow horse chestnut, 151

*Albizia julibrissin*, Acacia, acasse, 161

*Amorpha: caerulia* [*caerulea*], Bastard indigo, 151; *Amorpha fruticosa*, Bastard indigo, 151

*Amygdalus: persica, flore pleno* [*Prunus persica, flore pleno*], double-flowered peach, 152; *pumila, flore pleno* [*Prunus pumila, flore pleno*], sand or dwarf cherry, dwarf double-flowering almond, 153

*Andromeda exilaris* [*axillaris*], bog rosemary, 152, 158

*Aristolochia sipho.* [*Aristolochia macrophylla*], Dutchman's pipe, 154

*Arundo donax*, Maiden Cane, 153, 159

*Asiminia triloba*, pawpaw, 161

# B

*Baccharis* [prob. *Baccharis halimifolia*], prob. groundsel tree, 146

*Berberis canadensis*, barberry, 145

*Betula (alnus) maritima* [*Alnus maritima, betula*], sea-side alder, 153

*Bignonia: crucigera*, cross vine, trumpet flower, 153; *Bignonia semper virens*, yellow jasmine, 153

*Buxus: aureis* [*aureus*], gilded boxwood, 145, 155; *sempervirens arborescens*, tree boxwood, 161; *sempervirens suffruticosa*, edging boxwood, 161

# C

*Callicarpa americana*, Bermudas mulberry, French mulberry, American beautyberry, 154

*Calycanthus floridus*, sweet shrub of Carolina; Carolina allspice, 145, 155

*Carpinus ostrya*, hop tree, Horn Beam, 148

*Carya: illinoinensis*, pecan, 161; *laciniosa*, hickory, shellbark, 161; *ovata*, hickory, 161

*Castanea dentata*, common chestnut, 161

*Catalpa bignonioides*, catalpa, 161

*Cercis canadensis*, redbud, 161

*Chionanthus virginica*, fringe tree, 161

*Citisus laburnum* [*Cytisus laburnum, Laburnum anagyroides*], golden-chain, 153

*Clethra alnifolia*, clethra, sweet pepperbush, 148

*Colutia* [*Colutea*] *arborescens*, bladder senna, 152, 158

*Cornus: alba*, swamp dogwood, 152; *florida*, dogwood, 161; *mascula* [or *mas*], Cornelian cherry, 149

*Corylus: avellana*, cobb nuts, 161; *maxima*, filbert, 161

*Crataegus/Crategus/Craetagus: aria*, hawthorn, 153; *punctata*, large-berried thorn, 161; *spathulata*, small-berried thorn, 161

*Cupressus: disticha*, bald cyprus, 148; *sempervirens*, cypress, pyramidal, 161

# D

*Daphne mezerium* [*mezereum*], mezereon; paradise plant, 145, 155

*Dirca palustris*, leather bark, 146

# E

*Euonimus atrapurpurius* [*Euonymus atropurpureus*], burning bush, 157

*Evonimus americanus* [*Euonymus americanus*], spindle tree, 151

*Evonimus atrapurpurous* [*Euonymus atropurpureus*], burning bush, 146

# F

*Fothergilla gardeni* [*i*], dwarf fothergilla, dwarf witchalder, 146

*Franklinia alatamaha*, Franklin tree, 146, 157

*Fraxinus americana*, ash, 161

# G

*Gelseminum sempervirens*, yellow jessamine, 161

*Gleditsia triacanthos*, honey locust, 161

*Glycine frutescens* [*Wisteria frutescens*], kidney bean tree, wisteria, 149

*Gymnocladus dioicus*, Kentucky coffee tree, 161

# H

*H* [*ypericum*] *Angustifolium*, shrub St. John's wort, 145

*Halesia tetraptera* [or *carolina*], Carolina silverbell, 146, 157

*Hibiscus: coccineus*, scarlet rosemallow, 153; *syriacus*, althea tree, 161

*Hura crepitans*, sandbox tree, 161

*Hydrangea quercifolia*, hydrangea, 161; *Hydrangia* [*Hydrangea*] *arborescens*, 152, 158

## S

*Sabal unbraculifera*, royal palmetto, 161
*Salix: alba vitellina*, yellow willow, 161; *babylonica*, weeping willow, 161; *variegata*, 151
*Sambucus rubra* [*Sambucus canadensis*], American elder, sweet elder, 152
*Sassafras albidum*, sassafras, 161
*Sorbus: aucuparia*, European mountain ash, 148, 157; *sativa* [prob. *Sorbus domestica*], prob. service tree, 148, 157
*Stewartia malachodendron*, silky Stewartia or stuartia, 148, 157
*Styrax grandifolium*, snow-drop tree, snowbell, storax, 148, 157
*Swietenia mahogani*, mahogany, 161
*Syringa: persica*, Persian lilac, Persian jessamine, 154, 161; *vulgaris*, lilac, 161

## T

*Taxus: baccata*, yew, 161; *procumbens*, yew, 145, 155
*Thuja: occidentalis*, American arborvitae, white cedar, 146; *orientalis*, Oriental arborvitae, 149
*Tilia americana*, linden, 161
*Tsuga Canadensis*, hemlock, 161

## U

*Ulex europeus*, furze, 145, 155
*Ulmus americana*, elm, 161

## V

*Viburnum: alnifolium* [*Viburnum lantanoides*], hobble bush, 148, 157; *arboreum*, 148; *opulifolium*, 146, 157; *opulus*, Guelder rose, 161; *prunifolium*, blackhaw, 161

## Y

*Yucca: filamentosa*, Adam's needle, 151; *gloriosa*, Spanish dagger, 151

## Z

*Zanthorhiza apiifolia* [*Xanthorhiza simplicissima*], Yellow root, in Carola, 146

# Image Credits

The Mount Vernon Ladies' Association is grateful to the following individuals and institutions for providing illustrations on the pages listed here.

Gavin Ashworth: 10, 18, 33 (left), 38, 107, 110 (gatefold), 191, back cover

Courtesy Collection of the National Society of the Colonial Dames of America in the State of Maryland, Mount Clare Museum House: 25 (top)

Eric Benson: 4 (bottom, all), 76

Ron Blunt: 125

Courtesy Trustees of the Boston Public Library, Boston, Print Department, gift of the Massachusetts Society of Colonial Dames of America and the Warren-Prescott Chapter, Daughters of the American Revolution: 94

Renée Comet Photography: front cover (lower right), 30, 54, 98

Harry Connolly: 112, 138

Hal Conroy: 37, 77

Cameron Davidson|© Aerialstock.com: x, 132, 140–41

Courtesy Dietrich American Foundation, Philadelphia: 142

James Dunlop: 48

Mark Finkenstaedt: iv, 43, 117, 139

Russell Flint: 35, 135

Courtesy Gilcrease Museum, Tulsa, Okla.: 25 (right)

Courtesy UK Government Art Collection, London © Crown copyright: 33 (right)

Mark Gulezian: ii, 121 (bottom)

Patrick J. Hendrickson: 16

John Henley: front cover (top, lower left, lower center), endpapers, vi, ix, xv, 7, 14–15, 23, 26, 29, 69, 78–79, 101, 102, 106, 108–9, 110, 113, 119, 126, 128, 131, 162–63, 164, front and back dust jacket flaps

Jeanne Higbee: 70

Courtesy The Huntington Library, San Marino, Calif.: 20

Courtesy Independence National Historical Park, Philadelphia: 150

Amanda Isaac: 21

Courtesy John Bartram Association, Philadelphia: 25 (bottom)

Paul Kennedy: 36, 38, 123, verso of back endpaper

Courtesy Library of Congress, Washington, D.C.: 92, 147, 156

Courtesy Library of Virginia, Richmond: 121 (top)

Courtesy Maryland Historical Society, Baltimore: (1960.108.1.2.13) 13, (1960.108.1.2.10) 105

Dan Meyers: 25 (top)

J. Dean Norton: 6, 44, 51, 56, 60, 63, 66 (both), 67, 134

Edward Owen: verso of front endpaper, 2, 129

Courtesy Walter Gibson Peter III: 139

Karen Price: 80 (left), 84 (all), 104, 120

Robert Shenk: 31, 73, 115, 116, 124

Ted Vaughan: 62

Courtesy Washington-Custis-Lee Collection, University Collections of Art and History, Washington and Lee University, Lexington, Va.: 11

Esther C. White: 74 (all), 80 (right), 81, 83

Courtesy Winterthur Museum, Garden, and Library, Wilmington, Del., gift of Henry Francis du Pont, 1964.2201: xvi (cropped)

*George Washington's brass sundial sat atop a wooden post at the center of the carriage circle on the west side of the Mansion.*

*First Edition, 2015*

Published in the United States by the Fred W. Smith
National Library for the Study of George Washington for
the Mount Vernon Ladies' Association
P.O. Box 110
Mount Vernon, Virginia 22121

*The Fred W. Smith National Library for the Study of George Washington serves
the educational and academic mission of the Mount Vernon Ladies' Association,
which is to teach the widest public audience about the life, leadership, and legacy
of George Washington.*

Distributed by University of Virginia Press
Charlottesville, Virginia 22904
1-434-924-3468
www.upress.virginia.edu

*Library of Congress Cataloging-in-Publication Data*
Erby, Adam T.
    The general in the garden : George Washington's landscape at
Mount Vernon / essays by Adam T. Erby, J. Dean Norton, Esther C.
White ; Susan P. Schoelwer, editor ; foreword by Andrea Wulf.
        pages cm
    Includes bibliographical references and index.
    ISBN 978-0-931917-48-6
    1. Mount Vernon Gardens (Va.) 2. Mount Vernon (Va. : Estate) 3.
Washington, George, 1732–1799—Homes and haunts—Virginia—
Mount Vernon (Estate) 4. Landscape design—Virginia—Mount
Vernon (Estate)—History—18th century. I. Norton, J. Dean. II. White,
Esther C. III. Schoelwer, Susan Prendergast, editor. IV. Mount Vernon
Ladies' Association of the Union. V. Title.
    E312.5.E73 2014
    975.5'291—dc23
                            2013047173

*Book and jacket design:* Julia Sedykh Design
*Manuscript editor:* Phil Freshman
*Managing editor:* Stephen A. McLeod
*Proofreaders:* Phil Freshman, Michael Kane, and
    Stephen A. McLeod
*Indexer:* Monica S. Rumsey
*Printing and binding:* C&C Offset Printing Co., Ltd.,
    China

This book was typeset in MVB Verdigris.

FACING PAGE i: *John Ramage's 1789 portrait miniature
of George Washington.*

FRONTISPIECE: *Jean-Antoine Houdon's 1785 clay bust
of George Washington.*

PAGE iv: *Copper watering can used at Mount Vernon in
the 18th century.*

FACING THIS PAGE: *James Peale's 1796 portrait miniature of Martha Washington.*

ENDPAPERS: *Verdant lawn grass at Mount Vernon.*

DUST JACKET FLAPS: *Red-brick walls enclose garden
spaces at Mount Vernon.*

BACK COVER: *Landscape artist William Russell Birch
made this watercolor view of the Mansion's east front
around 1801–3. It served as the source for many prints by
Birch and other artists.*